Russ Alan Prince

Gary L. Rathbun

Arthur A. Bavelas

WEALTH PRESERVATION FOR PHYSICIANS

ADVANCED PLANNING FOR AFFLUENT DOCTORS

Wealth Preservation for Physicians:
Advanced Planning for Affluent Doctors

by Russ Alan Prince, Gary L. Rathbun and Arthur A. Bavelas

WEALTH MANAGEMENT PRESS

9800 Metcalf Avenue
Overland Park, KS 66212

ISBN number: 1-59969-005-5

Library of Congress control number: 2005911163

To Jeffrey and Jeffrey
Thank you for all the years of friendship.
Russ Alan Prince

———————————

To my wife Nancy
The definition of my true wealth.
Gary L. Rathbun

———————————

To my parents Andrew and Calliope
For always being there for our family in so many meaningful ways.
Arthur A. Bavelas

WEALTH PRESERVATION FOR PHYSICIANS

ADVANCED PLANNING FOR AFFLUENT DOCTORS

Table of Contents

ABOUT THE AUTHORS

RUSS ALAN PRINCE

Russ Alan Prince is president of the market research and consulting firm Prince & Associates, Inc., and a leading authority on the private wealth industry. Mr. Prince consults with the affluent on accessing various advanced planning services. He also works with financial and legal experts who provide cutting-edge strategies and concepts to the exceptionally wealthy. Mr. Prince is a columnist with various publications and is the author of more than 34 books focused on the high net worth market, including *Advanced Planning for the Ultra-Affluent: A Framework for Professional Advisors* (Institutional Investor) and *Inside the Family Office: Managing the Fortunes of the Exceptionally Wealthy* (Wealth Management Press).

GARY L. RATHBUN

pwcltd@privatewealth.net

Gary Rathbun is president and CEO of Private Wealth Consultants, Ltd., an internationally recognized wealth management firm. Private Wealth Consultants, Ltd., specializes in working with high net worth individuals, professionals and owners of closely held businesses. He is co-author of three books: *The Perfect Legacy*, *Wealth Accumulation for Dentists* and *Giving Wisely*.

ARTHUR A. BAVELAS

Arthur Bavelas is CEO of Resource Network, Ltd., a leading wealth management firm catering to affluent individuals and family offices. Accessing renowned authorities from the financial and legal communities, he coordinates their actions, bringing state-of-the-art concepts and strategies, as well as unique opportunities, to high net worth individuals.

Foreword

WEALTH PRESERVATION FOR PHYSICIANS

ADVANCED PLANNING

FOR AFFLUENT DOCTORS

For over 20 years I have worked with many physicians, helping them build better practices and better lives. During that time I have read hundreds of articles and dozens of books on various subjects dealing with the major financial issues these doctors face every day. Throughout all of this reading, I rarely come across anything that is truly worth the physicians' time to study, let alone apply to their situations.

In addition, most of the books try to be the final authority on all of the subjects that affect the physician. *Wealth Preservation for Physicians: Advanced Planning for Affluent Doctors* is different. The authors have tapped into the expertise of several top advisors around the country who specialize in a particular area of wealth preservation.

The authors provide perspective about both the world of the affluent physician and the field of advanced planning. When they deal with specifics, each subject is both detailed and yet brief. There is enough information to inform readers and let them know if this strategy is appropriate for their situations, yet not so cumbersome to confuse and lose the readers. As Goldilocks said, "this one is just right!"

This book offers useful guidance to physicians who want to plan for their financial security, whether they are in the early stage of their careers, well established or getting ready to retire. It is particularly valuable because it addresses many of the potential risks and issues that are unique to affluent physicians.

One of the most interesting aspects of this primer is that it utilized exclusive research provided by Russ Alan Prince of Prince & Associates. Russ has established himself as one of the premier experts on the financial needs and strategies of the affluent. This research provides the reader with actual opinions and concerns of colleagues around the country.

I know that you will enjoy reading through *Wealth Preservation for Physicians: Advanced Planning for Affluent Doctors*, and I am sure that it will help you in your decisions going forward.

Alan Himmelstein
Hospital Care Consultant
San Antonio, Texas

October 2005

ABOUT THIS BOOK: WEALTH PRESERVATION FOR PHYSICIANS

This book was written at the prompting of a number of our affluent-physician clients as well as the executives who manage their medical practices. They wanted a primer on the nature of advanced planning and how some of the strategies can be used to preserve their wealth.

———————————

A career as a physician can prove exceptionally rewarding especially from the perspective of helping others and making a societal difference. However, the financial benefits of being a physician have diminished considerably over the last five, ten or fifteen years. Moreover, it's most likely that these financial benefits are going to diminish more before they get any better—if they ever do get better, which is certainly in question.

Although the overwhelming majority of physicians will never get "rich," for those who are wealthy and anticipate becoming wealthy, there is a deep concern for preserving their wealth. When it comes to wealth preservation, we're very clear about what this means for affluent physicians. We're talking about ways to ensure the safeguarding of a physician's net worth by defending and often increasing his or her net worth in the face of many who seek to share it. Among the likely participants who seek to share an affluent physician's wealth, we include:

- The government, with its "aggressive" taxing power
- Malpractice litigants who are oft times prompted to sue when anything does not turn out perfectly, irrespective if the physician is at fault or not
- Non-malpractice litigants such as ex-spouses, ex-business associates and everyone who thinks all physicians are fabulously wealthy and chooses to target them with unjust lawsuits

Another facet of wealth preservation is protecting and efficaciously facilitating practice ownership among physicians. It's an industry norm for physicians to lose significant monies when physician partners die and spouses inherit their equity in the practice, or when physicians get hurt and are unable to work yet still have a stake in the practice. These scenarios can be addressed so that they do not cause the financial disasters that are so common today.

Making sure an affluent physician's wealth is distributed in the most tax-wise manner to the people and organizations he or she desires is yet another facet of wealth preservation. The vast majority of affluent physicians prefer to avoid handing monies to the government when it's not "necessary" to do so. Wealth preservation in this context begins by ensuring the hard-earned wealth of affluent physicians remains in their hands or is bestowed to the people and organizations they care about.

What is important to realize is that the approach to wealth preservation we're dealing with here is not focused on finding winning investments. It's not about becoming affluent, it's about staying affluent. Although investing is a component of some of the wealth-preservation strategies we bring to physicians, those investments are usually "set" and therefore, out of the control of the physician. This is in contrast to a qualified retirement plan or a discretionary investment portfolio, where the physician can have a say in the investments. Monies placed in a captive insurance company, for example, must be managed within a very strict set of parameters. Therefore, input from physicians on how to manage these monies is a nonissue.

The methodology for wealth preservation that we will be discussing is predicated on advanced planning. The ability to navigate through the tax code and astutely maneuver through the legal and regulatory environments enabling us to capitalize on nuances in the laws and rules with strategies and financial products is the state-of-the-art nature of advanced planning. Without question, advanced planning—wealth enhancement, estate planning, asset-protection planning and charitable giving—often proves to be very profitable for physicians. In this book the focus will be squarely on advanced planning wealth-preservation strategies that principally entail estate and asset-protection planning.

The physicians we almost universally work with are affluent, which we define as having a net worth of $5 million or more. However, many of the strategies we utilize can benefit less wealthy physicians, although some strategies necessitate greater private wealth and are therefore only applicable to affluent physicians.

Moving beyond affluent physicians as individuals, advanced planning is often appropriate for medical practices. A medical practice can be anything from a single practitioner to a large hospital where the physicians are employees. When engaging in advanced planning with medical practices, we're leveraging the corporate structure to provide wealth-preservation strategies. When we work with medical practices, physicians at all levels of net worth can benefit.

The strategies that constitute advanced planning are ever evolving in lockstep with the perpetual modifications and adjustments in the tax code, regulatory environment and the world of financial innovations. Many of the strategies we bring to affluent physicians tend to be on the exotic side. Having said this, it's critical to recognize that, for us, there are no shades of gray. Everything we propose, everything we do, is composed of "bright-line transactions." In a nutshell, everything we do is *perfectly legal* and *completely ethical*.

What This Book Will *Not* Do for Affluent Physicians and Their Practices

After reading this book, no one should expect to be able to identify, develop, customize or implement advanced planning strategies. No one, after reading this book, will be able to go out and practice as an advanced planner. The ability, for instance, to exploit a nuance in the tax code and consequently save a wealthy physician hundreds of thousands of dollars in taxes, or the ability to employ a captive insurance company to mitigate the cost of malpractice insurance for a group of surgeons and simultaneously create for them a future source of income is a specialty—the purview of the advanced planner.

If an affluent physician or a medical practice is at all interested in the benefits of advanced planning, especially when we're dealing with the more esoteric legal and financial strategies and products, then the services of an advanced planner is a necessity.

What This Book Will Do for Affluent Physicians and Their Practices

In writing this book we wanted to:
- *Look at the world of the affluent physician.* First, we will provide perspective by constructing an analytic model to size the universe of affluent physicians. Then we will drill down—based on a national study of affluent physicians—on their sources of financial dissatisfaction.
- *Provide a brief overview of advanced planning.* As noted, advanced planning is not investment management, nor is it retirement planning. Advanced planning is a way to make the most of the regulatory and tax system to maximize wealth retention without ever going over the line. Very importantly, we include a warning as well as detailed the guidelines and steps for selecting and working with a high-quality advanced planner.

- *Exemplify some of the more commonly employed advanced planning strategies for wealth preservation.* Our intent is to furnish a succinct synopsis of a handful of the more easily applicable strategies. Therefore, we have only provided a broad but precise explanation of some advanced planning strategies. We intentionally decided not to discuss the more esoteric strategies, as their application requires a very precise situation thereby making them inappropriate for most affluent physicians. Additionally, they tend to have exceptional complexity, making it hard to do justice to them and be succinct.

As we noted, this book is a primer—an introduction to the use of advanced planning to preserve the wealth of affluent physicians (and less wealthy physicians under the proper circumstances). We understand that by being attuned to what is happening in the field of medicine, being knowledgeable about advanced planning, and having a broad-based conceptual understanding of selected strategies, affluent physicians will be able make informed decisions that can result in significant wealth perpetuation.

PART I

THE AFFLUENT
PHYSICIAN

43,700 Affluent Physicians Control $374.3 Billion

Making money is one of the cardinal American virtues, right up there with freedom of speech and the vote, and seldom before have so many people so fully and successfully exercised their right to wealth as they have at the turn of the twenty-first century. Although the practice of medicine in and of itself does not often translate into personal fortunes, the ability to generate significant cash flows and to invest those cash flows can produce millionaire physicians. Furthermore, there are those physicians who marry their expertise and talents with a creative spark and produce innovations or obtain equity positions in medical ventures that in turn make them wealthy.

Let's begin by getting our hands around what we mean by "affluent physician." Also, let's look at how they made their fortunes as well as how many of these wealthy physicians are out there.

Defining an Affluent Physician

First we must define what we mean by an affluent physician. There are many ways physicians can become wealthy, with some of those ways having nothing to do with medicine. However, for purposes of this book an affluent physician is one who:

- *Is practicing.* He or she is seeing patients today.
- *Has a minimum net worth of $5 million.* These are all the physician's assets minus all of his or her liabilities.
- *Is self-made.* The physician became a millionaire based on his or her own efforts. He or she did not inherit the money.

An affluent physician has created private wealth by any combination of the following:

- *Generating significant incomes from his or her medical practice.* This usually means he or she is in a high-income specialty such as neurosurgery, and over time these monies added up.
- *Investing well.* From purchasing a home that has meaningfully appreciated, to prudent stock market investments, to private equity positions, to even artwork, the physician has leveraged his or her income. The investment can also have been made in the physician's medical group and ancillary or related medical services and/or products.
- *Leveraging his or her expertise into equity participation in products, services or firms.* From physicians who own patents to those who capitalized on their knowledge and talents for equity in medical business ventures, these physicians can end up quite wealthy.

Although a solid income over time can enable some physicians to achieve a net worth of $5 million or more, often physicians must also have a strong investment portfolio. On the other hand, physicians who leverage their expertise need not have outstanding incomes or investments that meaningfully appreciate; these are the physicians who tend to be the wealthiest.

Analytic Modeling

Just how many practicing physicians have a net worth of $5 million or more? To determine this, Prince & Associates, Inc., developed an analytical model to calculate the number of affluent physicians.

Sizing the affluent universe is daunting. There is no master list, and many affluent physicians understandably prefer anonymity to ward off bothersome solicitations and to protect their privacy. As a result, we turned to analytic modeling to size and scope the world of wealthy physicians.

Analytic modeling is one of several methodologies used to estimate what cannot be directly measured. Because the methodology we employed is but one way of generating estimates, however, we validated its results against other modeling techniques.

At its core, analytic modeling uses a multi-equation approach to create scenarios or best estimates of the number of affluent physicians across predetermined, asset-sized segments. In this case, the analytic model was constructed of a series of equations resulting in deterministic algorithms.

There are two areas to examine closely when evaluating the output of an analytic model such as this. The first is the quality of the data incorporated into the model. We addressed this threat by closely examining each data point, requiring multiple confirmations before including them in the model.

The other potential threat to validity is the assumption made about how core measures interact, because a change in structural relationships can have a cascading effect on the calculations. We approached this issue by creating scenarios where the core measures were systematically manipulated. During this process we conducted sensitivity analyses to provide a better understanding of the likelihood of each conclusion.

The Number of Affluent Physicians and Their Aggregate Wealth

This model was an extension of previous analytic models we developed to ascertain the size and scope of the private wealth in the world today. With respect to physicians, we started with a universe of about 890,000 physicians and ended up with a best estimate of 43,700 affluent physicians in total. Our low-end estimate concludes that there are 28,800 affluent physicians, and our high-end estimate puts the number at 51,600 (Exhibit 1.1).

Exhibit 1.1 | The Number of Affluent Physicians

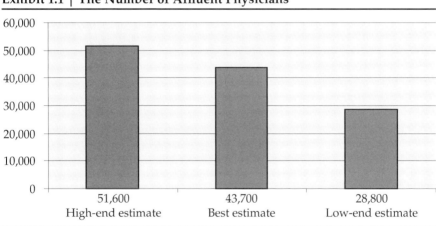

| | 51,600 | 43,700 | 28,800 |
| | High-end estimate | Best estimate | Low-end estimate |

Moving beyond the number of affluent physicians, we calculated their aggregate net worth (Exhibit 1.2). In effect, what is the value of the net assets controlled by affluent physicians? Our high-end estimate places their aggregate net worth at $476.8 billion. The low-end estimate is $208.3 billion. But our best estimate is $374.3 billion.

Exhibit 1.2 | The Net Worth of Affluent Physicians

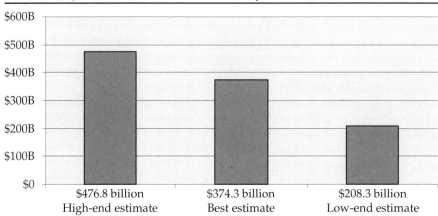

$476.8 billion	$374.3 billion	$208.3 billion
High-end estimate	Best estimate	Low-end estimate

Conclusion

Compared to the world at large and other professionals, there are a significant number of affluent physicians who have a significant amount of private wealth. Using analytic modeling, our best estimate is that there are 43,700 affluent physicians. In the total their net worth is $374.3 billion. And, as we will see, for a variety of reasons, they tend to be dissatisfied with their financial situations.

SOURCES OF FINANCIAL
DISSATISFACTION AMONG
AFFLUENT PHYSICIANS

Affluent physicians, as compared to their peers, are distinguished by their wealth. At the same time, they face many of the same conundrums confronting their professional peers as well as additional issues brought about by their success. Now, we have yet to meet an affluent physician who prefers less money to more. It's just that the additional wealth creates its own concerns—and opportunities.

Moving beyond our experience working with affluent physicians and their practices in maximizing their wealth, we conducted a national survey of 941 affluent physicians. To be included in the survey, an affluent physician had to meet the criteria set forth in the previous chapter.

Our objective was to gain greater perspective on the world of affluent physicians—in particular some of their key personal and practice concerns—as well as their experiences and actions surrounding the field of advanced planning. With respect to advanced planning, the data is cited as appropriate throughout the book. In this chapter, we will drill down on the sources of financial dissatisfaction among affluent physicians. However, before doing so, let's get an idea of the methodology involved in surveying affluent physicians.

Sampling Methodology

In studying the wealthy we cannot engage in classic probability sampling. Quite the opposite: We employed a nonprobability sampling process commonly referred to as snowball sampling. Why did we take this approach? Simply put, there are not any lists of affluent physicians as we have defined them. Moreover, even if such a list existed, motivating them to fill out a questionnaire is another matter. Snowball sampling is used when the targeted audience—in this case affluent physicians—cannot be cost-effectively reached by classic probability sampling.

When conducting research in this universe, the method of data collection is extremely important, which is why a highly trained and experienced interviewer surveyed each affluent physician. As for motivating the affluent physicians to participate, each one was provided with a $300 honorarium. In the end, our sample consisted of 941 affluent physicians with an aggregate net worth of $8.3 billion.

Net Worth

All the physicians we surveyed were practicing, had a minimum net worth of $5 million, and were self-made. Although we set the bar at $5 million, the surveyed physicians tended to be wealthier.

The great majority of them (84.3 percent) had a net worth between $5 million and $10 million. The net worth of the remaining 15.7 percent exceeded $10 million (Exhibit 2.1).

Exhibit 2.1 | Net Worth

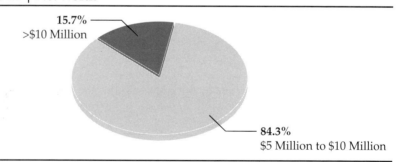

15.7%
>$10 Million

84.3%
$5 Million to $10 Million

N = 941 Affluent Physicians

It's important to note that all these physicians have been practicing for more than fifteen years and that 88.5 percent are older than 45 (Exhibit 2.2). Moreover, all but one of the physicians with a net worth over $10 million were over 45 years old. That physician's considerable wealth, which is in excess of $40 million, is primarily a function of the revenues from patents. Overall, it's not surprising, based on our definition of an affluent physician, that their years of practicing medicine are critical to them becoming wealthy.

Exhibit 2.2 | Age

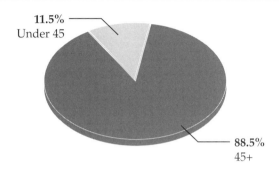

11.5%
Under 45

88.5%
45+

N = 941 Affluent Physicians

Financial Dissatisfaction

We evaluated the level of financial satisfaction among the affluent physicians surveyed. Across the board, no one was completely satisfied with his or her financial situation. Each affluent physician was dissatisfied to some degree. Moreover, nearly three out of five physicians (58.1 percent) were highly dissatisfied. A third (33.8 percent) were moderately dissatisfied. The remaining 8.1 percent were somewhat dissatisfied (Exhibit 2.3).

Exhibit 2.3 | Dissatisfied with Their Financial Situations

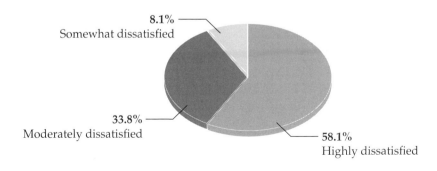

8.1%
Somewhat dissatisfied

33.8%
Moderately dissatisfied

58.1%
Highly dissatisfied

N = 941 Affluent Physicians

When we examine the dissatisfaction findings by our net worth segments, we see that there is greater overall dissatisfaction among the less wealthy physicians (Exhibit 2.4). For example, 13.5 percent of the physicians with a net worth greater than $10 million are somewhat dissatisfied compared to 7.1 percent of physicians with a net worth between $1 million and $10 million. Also, proportionately fewer of the wealthier physicians are highly dissatisfied (48.7 percent compared to 59.9 percent).

Exhibit 2.4 | Less Wealthy Physicians are More Dissatisfied

	$1M to $10M	>$10M
Highly dissatisfied	59.9%	48.7%
Moderately dissatisfied	33.0%	37.8%
Somewhat dissatisfied	7.1%	13.5%

N = 941 Affluent Physicians

In delving deeper into this matter, we have found that those physicians with truly significant wealth (more than $20 million in net worth) tend to be less dissatisfied with their financial situations. And by definition they are in the wealthier segment.

Sources of Financial Dissatisfaction

With so many affluent physicians dissatisfied with their financial situations, we then sort to understand why this is the case. Using a statistical methodology known as factor analysis, we identified the primary sources of physician financial dissatisfaction. We uncovered four principal sources. They are:

- rules and regulations negatively affecting the profitability of the practice
- excessive and increasing liability
- downward pressure on incomes
- financial fragility

From a structural perspective, the sources of financial dissatisfaction work from "lowest" to "highest." That is, the impact of each factor is cumulative. All the physicians who are concerned with excessive and increasing liability are also concerned with downward pressure on incomes and so forth. Hence, we will look at each of these factors in ascending order of importance.

Rules and Regulations Negatively Affecting the Profitability of the Practice. From capitation to mountains of paperwork, affluent physicians have to spend more in order to make their practices work, and this is a major concern of 77.5 percent of them (Exhibit 2.5). Proportionately more of the less affluent physicians (79.1 percent) see the financial burden imposed by these rules and regulations, compared to 68.9 percent of the wealthier physicians.

Exhibit 2.5 | Very Concerned About the Negative Impact of Rules and Regulations

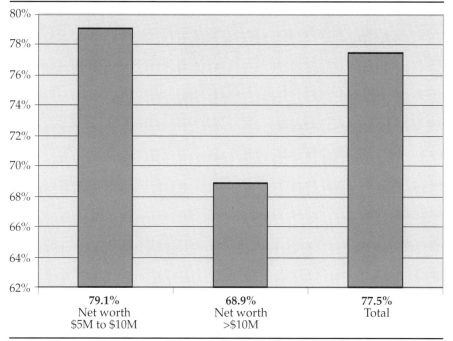

N = 941 Affluent Physicians

One of the major costs associated with these rules and regulations is the ability to attract, retain and motivate key personnel. These people are the ones who often need to understand the rules and regulations and manage the practice accordingly. In these situations, medical practices might want to consider establishing deferred compensation plans or other types of executive benefit programs. Another option is to create controlled forward-funding entities that can be employed to give bonuses these employees. The advantage of this approach is that the monies placed in these entities can grow tax deferred until they are needed.

What's more, 85.3 percent of the affluent physicians only expect the situation to deteriorate further (Exhibit 2.6). This was the case for both the wealthier (82.4 percent) and less wealthy physicians (85.9 percent). Generally, speaking, they see the regulatory environment becoming harsher and therefore a greater drag on the profitability of their practices.

Exhibit 2.6 | The Regulatory Environment Will Worsen

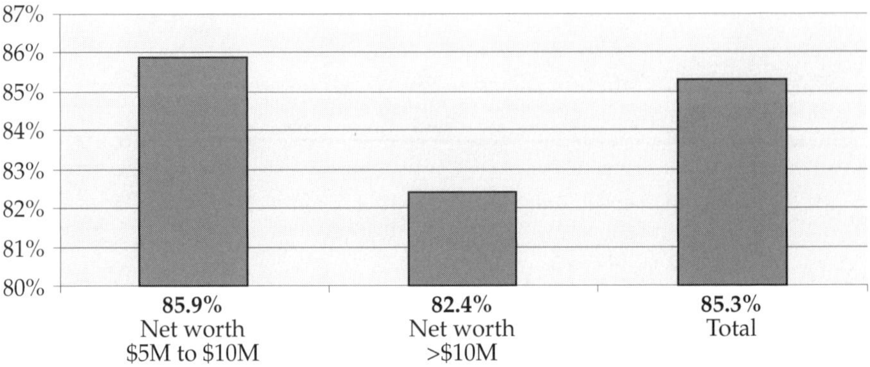

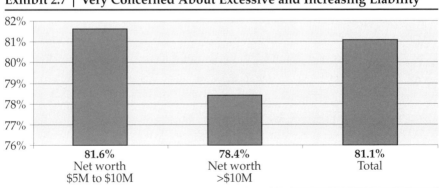

87%
86%
85%
84%
83%
82%
81%
80%
85.9%
Net worth
$5M to $10M
82.4%
Net worth
>$10M
85.3%
Total

N = 941 Affluent Physicians

Excessive and Increasing Liability. Although physicians are more than ever handcuffed when it comes to aspects of the way they practice, they are still held responsible. Even with managed care, physicians are still responsible for the ongoing delivery of quality healthcare but in many ways do not control how that care is delivered. Hence, managed care can put physicians in an even worse position when it comes to the potential for being sued for malpractice. For many physicians, this is forcing a more defensive approach to the practice of medicine. It is also evident in the "per physician" increasing number of malpractice suits filed each year.

About four out of five affluent physicians (81.1 percent) are tremendously concerned by liability issues (Exhibit 2.7). This was seen more among less wealthy physicians (81.6 percent), because a lawsuit could potentially be more damaging to the finances of the less wealthy physicians.

Exhibit 2.7 | Very Concerned About Excessive and Increasing Liability

82%
81%
80%
79%
78%
77%
76%
81.6%
Net worth
$5M to $10M
78.4%
Net worth
>$10M
81.1%
Total

N = 941 Affluent Physicians

We found that 82.0 percent of affluent physicians believe the liability problem will become more problematic in the next two years (Exhibit 2.8). The difference between the wealthier and less wealthy physicians was negligible as the anticipation of a more difficult liability environment was a function of the physician's specialty. What is clear is that liability is likely to be a growing problem for all physicians.

Exhibit 2.8 | The Liability Situation Will Worsen in the Next Two Years

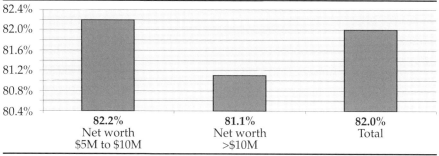

N = 941 Affluent Physicians

Although politicians talk about solutions, such as capping awards and tort reform, this has so far provided little in the way of comfort for physicians. In fact, only 8.5 percent of physicians believe that meaningful tort reform will actually occur in the next two years (Exhibit 2.9). The less wealthy physicians (9.1 percent) are more optimistic that their wealthier brethren (5.4 percent). And by *meaningful tort reform* they are referring to consequential changes that will translate into lower malpractice premiums.

Exhibit 2.9 | Meaningful Tort Reform is Coming

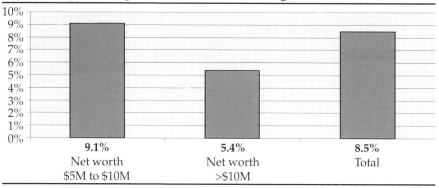

N = 941 Affluent Physicians

Liability concerns both within their profession and outside of it are pro-viding the rationale and motivation for affluent physicians to take strong steps to protect their wealth (see Chapter 8, "Asset-Protection Planning") as well as look for ways to better deal with malpractice costs (see Chapter 10, "Leveraging Captive Insurance Companies").

Downward Pressure on Incomes. With the need to deal with costly rules and regulations, the costs of malpractice and a medical environment that tends to compensate physicians less as time goes on, 85.8 percent of affluent physicians are very concerned about downward pressure on their incomes (Exhibit 2.10). This sentiment is more prevalent among less wealthy physi-cians (86.9 percent compared to 79.7 percent) as they tend to be more depen-dent on their incomes to maintain their lifestyles.

Exhibit 2.10 | Very Concerned About Downward Pressure on Incomes

| | 86.9% | 79.7% | 85.8% |
| | Net worth $5M to $10M | Net worth >$10M | Total |

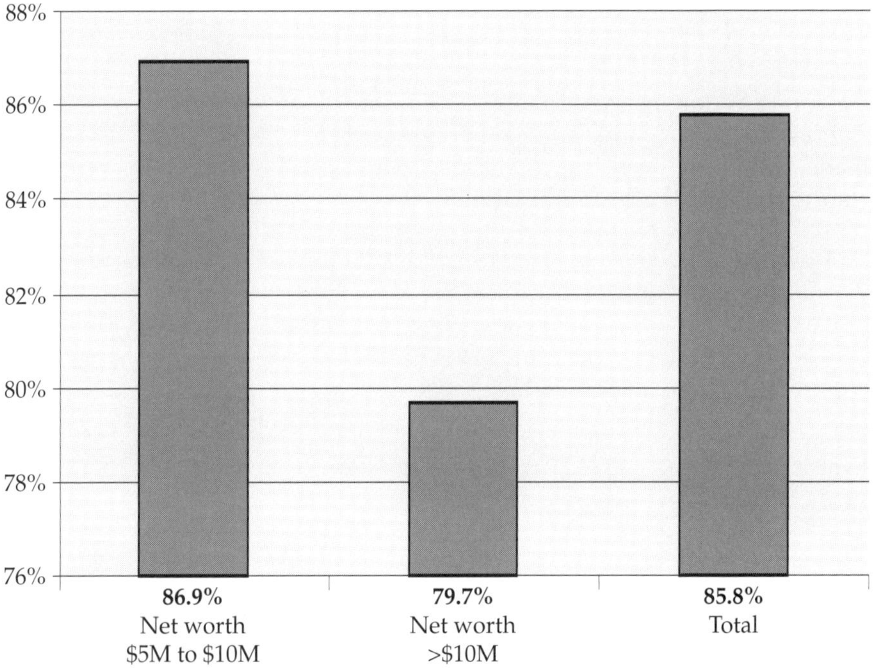

N = 941 Affluent Physicians

What we also discovered is that very few affluent physicians (6.8 percent) see a reversal in this trend (Exhibit 2.11). Proportionately more of the wealth-ier physicians expect incomes for physicians to rise (8.8 percent compared to 6.4 percent). The idea that physician incomes will turn around is anathema to the greater majority of affluent physicians.

Exhibit 2.11 | Physician Incomes Will Rise Significantly in Their Lifetimes

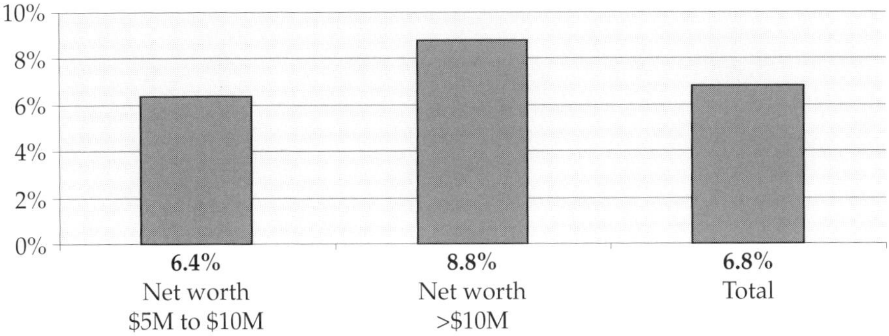

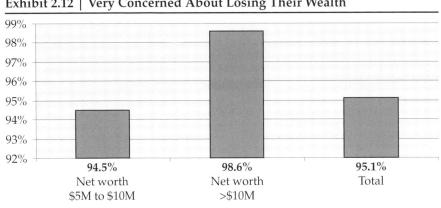

| 6.4% | 8.8% | 6.8% |
| Net worth $5M to $10M | Net worth >$10M | Total |

N = 941 Affluent Physicians

With physician incomes not expected to rise in a meaningful manner, we found that increasingly physicians are looking for viable and creative ways to preserve their wealth. Advanced planning proves to be one highly efficacious way to this accomplish this goal.

Plagued by Perceived Financial Fragility. As surely as fortunes have been made, they have been lost. A sharp downturn in the stock market, for instance, could deal a body blow to the net worth of someone who is overexposed on the equity side.

Nearly all the affluent physicians (95.1 percent) are concerned about losing their wealth with the wealthier ones proportionately more concerned (98.6 percent compared to 94.5 percent [Exhibit 2.12]). Once a physician has gotten used to being very well off, being less so can be hard to abide.

Exhibit 2.12 | Very Concerned About Losing Their Wealth

| 94.5% | 98.6% | 95.1% |
| Net worth $5M to $10M | Net worth >$10M | Total |

N = 941 Affluent Physicians

Aside from not being particularly interested in downsizing their lifestyles, our experience working with affluent physicians shows us that more than a few are engaging in a financial balancing act. Affluent physicians—as well as many other types of multimillionaires—are all too often only a few steps away from painful financial and lifestyle reversals. Consequently, they tend to worry greatly about making sure they maintain their fortunes.

This point is critical and is the driving force behind this book. It has taken these physicians years of hard work and often a little luck to achieve their current level of economic success. Furthermore, they realize they lack the time and in many cases, the energies, to recoup their wealth given a significant reversal of fortune. For most of them, today's medical environment also works against them in rebuilding their wealth if it was indeed lost. Additionally, they strongly prefer not to be forced to downgrade their present lifestyles. Put all this together and we find these affluent physicians are forcefully motivated to take steps to preserve the wealth that supports their way of life.

Conclusion

For the most part, affluent physicians are not very happy about their financial situations. Their biggest worries center on losing their wealth. They generally recognize that they do not have the time or the imminent opportunities to rebuild their fortunes if they were lost.

At the same time, affluent physicians see the financial benefits of their profession eroding. There is downward pressure on incomes that shows no signs of abating. Liability concerns are also intensifying with no signs of abating. And to complicate matters even more, the regulatory environment is seen as hostile, with more aggression on the way.

Overall, affluent physicians are metaphorically stuck between a rock and a hard place. In our experience, they want to go from preserving and directing their wealth to expanding it, and few have a good idea how to accomplish this feat. This is where advanced planning comes into play and where we now turn.

PART II

ADVANCED
PLANNING

3

THE NATURE OF
ADVANCED PLANNING

If the objective is wealth preservation, advanced planning can certainly fit the bill. Although advanced planning encompasses more than wealth preservation, we will focus our discussion on this topic. Advanced planning is a critical process that regularly results in the repositioning and restructuring of the assets of an affluent physician to preserve and magnify his or her wealth as best as possible.

As a process, advanced planning leverages the tax laws and regulations, often employing tax-driven, cutting-edge strategies and sophisticated financial products in unique ways for the benefit of physicians. It can be conceptualized as four interrelated sets of services (see below). Meanwhile, the critical process that is advanced planning is encapsulated in the Virtuous Cycle (see the next chapter for a discussion of the process).

Advanced planning differs from other types of financial services for affluent physicians. Advanced planning, for instance, is a subset of wealth management. The latter is a holistic approach to solving financial problems and is quite comprehensive, incorporating not only advanced planning but often the full array of credit products, discretionary investment management and retirement planning.

Advanced planning is an area of proficiency that is unto itself composed of an even more refined set of expertise. Although credit and investment management are sometimes incorporated into advanced planning strategies, they play a supporting role. Moreover, when they are part of an advanced planning strategy there is usually limited discretion on the part of the physician.

To better understand advanced planning, let's look at the four thematically interlocking advanced planning services. We will then touch on the Innovation Process and conclude with the eight core elements of advanced planning.

The Advanced Planning Services

The strategies of advanced planners can be characterized as *basic* and as *state-of-the-art*. The *basics* include the plethora of strategies that are readily recognized and generally applicable for most physicians including the more affluent ones. Just consider the case of malpractice insurance. For physicians, irrespective of the level of affluence, obtaining malpractice insurance is generally a wise move. This falls under the category of *basic*. However, when we address malpractice insurance by employing a captive insurance company that also potentially increases the wealth of the participating physicians, we have entered the realm of *state-of-the-art*.

When working with affluent physicians, our ability to adroitly apply the basics is a given. For a percentage of our affluent physician clients we have found that there is never a need or desire to move beyond the basics. In their situations, cutting-edge expertise is not being put to use nor should it be. However, we have found that when it comes to many other affluent physicians, the opportunities to employ state-of-the-art advanced planning strategies are in high demand. Moreover, in most cases, if the objective is the conservation of private wealth then it's often essential to selectively use these sophisticated strategies.

As noted, advanced planning entails leveraging the legal, tax and regulatory systems as well as the innovative use of financial products to provide one or more of four interrelated services:

- Wealth enhancement
- Estate planning
- Asset-protection planning
- Charitable giving

These four services interlock thematically and are important to varying degrees to affluent physicians, depending on each one's individual circumstances. Moreover, when engaging in advanced planning with affluent physicians, synergies are created among the four services. And the ability to profit from these synergies can meaningfully benefit the physician. As we are concentrating on wealth preservation—estate planning and asset-protection planning—it is valuable to note that there are considerable synergies between the two.

Let's now delve a little deeper into each of the four sets of advanced planning services.

Wealth Enhancement. With respect to asset management, the goal is to produce the best-possible investment performance. Affluent physicians, because they are willing to pay for advice and because they have money to invest, are clearly focused on returns. Unlike institutional investors such as pension funds and endowments, affluent physicians must also contend with taxes, and working to make the tax issues less of a drain on absolute returns is an important aspect of wealth enhancement. The key for the affluent physician is to determine the current timing, character and amount of taxable income.

When it comes to investment income, the ideal transition is from income to short-term capital gains, to long-term capital gains, to tax deferral and ultimately to no taxes whatsoever. This continuum drives the services of advanced planners, with the goal of moving the affluent-physician client situation as far along the continuum as is practicable under the given circumstances.

There is a wide variety of advanced planning strategies that can be utilized to enhance wealth. Although we are not intending to discuss wealth enhancement to any great degree, wealth enhancement is often a benefit of employing captive insurance companies. Additional examples of wealth enhancement include deferred compensation programs and a contingent swap designed to offset ordinary income and convert it into capital gains over a specified time. Advanced planners are able to enhance a physician's wealth significantly when the physician's practice can be integrated through dormant asset financing, synthetic equity strategies and a number of tax-favored programs that move money and/or benefits from the practice to the individual.

Estate Planning. As long as there are estate and gift taxes, as long as there are intergenerational considerations, and as long as there are interconnected practice interests, there will be a need for wealth-transfer strategies and tactics. When it comes to estate planning, advanced planners are called upon to facilitate not only the transfer of wealth in accord with the wishes of the affluent-physician client, but to do so in as tax-efficient a manner as possible within prescribed parameters.

It is quite possible, for example, to eliminate estate taxes. Achieving that goal could require the use of charitable instruments and the formal abrogation of control over selected assets. Such an approach proves of interest to a modest number of affluent physicians. Basic estate planning employing such strategies as revocable trusts and traditional life insurance is far from complicated and sufficient for some affluent physicians. For those affluent physicians with more money and more complicated financial pictures and goals, there are a number of more sophisticated approaches to wealth transfer, including self-canceling installment notes, cascading grantor-retained annuity trusts, intentionally defective trusts and remainder-purchase marital trusts. Some more affluent physicians, for example, can use a combination of techniques including dynasty trusts to avoid estate and gift taxes forever.

Estate planning also comes into play when action has to be taken to ensure the efficient and cost-effective transfer of a practice's ownership or assets. The forced transferring of equity in medical practices due to the death or disability of a partner proves to be a major way for affluent physicians to abrogate their wealth.

Asset-Protection Planning. Asset-protection planning is what protects an affluent physician's hard-earned wealth. There are a great many strategies that affluent physicians can employ to protect their wealth against potential creditors and litigants, children-in-law and potential ex-spouses. Which ones work best prove to be very situational.

Moving beyond the astute use of property and liability insurance, some of the strategies are quite rudimentary and predicated on dissociation, which occurs when the affluent physician transfers his or her assets to another person or entity while retaining access. Such strategies include transferring assets to a spouse, offshore trusts and self-settled spendthrift trusts.

Getting somewhat more sophisticated, with transformation strategies the assets of the affluent physician are converted into different assets that are much harder, if not impossible, for litigants to acquire. The homestead exemption, interests in limited partnerships or limited liability companies, and the selective use of life insurance and annuities are all examples of transformation strategies.

Monetization in conjunction with transformation and replication are at the very cutting edge of asset-protection strategies. Monetization strategies utilize forward contracts and complex installment sales whereas replication strategies benefit from derivatives to make assets disappear and subsequently reappear in entities beyond the reach of litigants. As a result, these strategies, if properly executed, will oblige a determined opponent to seek a compromise.

Charitable Giving. Apart from wealth and success, a strong majority of affluent physicians want to give something back. Charitable gifting can also be motivated by those who share Warren Buffett's philosophy of leaving children "enough money so they would feel they could do anything, but not so much that they could do nothing."

Although the motivations and values differ, charitable gifting is an important component in advanced planning, especially when coordinated with the other three services. Private foundations are a case in point. A family foundation serves a wide variety of functions but the transfer of wealth among family members is tangential, if applicable at all. Still, research clearly shows the enormous interest among the affluent in private foundations for a number of reasons having nothing to do with passing on assets to heirs.

When an affluent-physician client of ours is strongly philanthropic, that inclination can be coordinated to produce additional wealth enhancement and wealth-transfer strategies. Aside from private foundations with their specific limitations, supporting organizations and donor-advised funds allow for the maximum immediate tax benefits timed for the benefit of the physician. Charitable remainder trusts and charitable gift annuities provide both tax benefits and income streams. Charitable lead trusts can finesse the estate tax while passing wealth to future generations. Finally, although philanthropy does not coordinate strongly with asset protection, seeing assets go to charities rather than to litigants and creditors may produce some satisfaction.

The Innovation Process

The Innovation Process is the cerebral side of advanced planning and is central to our ability to deliver creative and powerful solutions for the financial and selected legal issues facing physicians today. The Innovation Process starts with evaluating where we are today and concludes with a viable strategy specifically suited to the world of affluent physicians.

The process is in many ways a search for nuance. It is often a matter of identifying a wrinkle in the tax code and knowing under what conditions affluent physicians can benefit. As such, the Innovation Process is often about developing methodologies and systems that can turn a breakthrough idea into a viable strategy or even a new financial product.

The Innovation Process is composed of four interconnected processes that can ensure state-of-the-art results.

- *Environmental scanning* entails keeping an eye out for new and emerging industry trends. Included here is an ongoing systematic evaluation of the evolving legal and regulatory landscape as well as the changing preferences and requirements of affluent physicians and their practices. Also, as part of environmental scanning, advanced planners are perpetually appraising the strategies and financial products that come onto their radar screens.

- *Scenario thinking* is envisioning where those trends might lead under certain situations. Scenarios are hypothetical futures that an affluent physician might encounter, and each scenario has a probability and a risk assessment associated with it. When applied to the Innovation Process, scenario thinking is used to develop a number of potentially viable strategies.

- *Actualization* is turning hypothetical ideas into real strategies and products. Everything that is required to make the idea work effectively is delineated and put in place. Often, this entails enlisting specialists like the ones coauthoring the chapters in Part III, "Selected Advanced Planning Wealth-Preservation Strategies."
- *Validation* encompasses implementing and regularly updating the innovation. Validation also encompasses two additional considerations: one legal or regulatory and the other ethical. On the legal/regulatory front, the advanced planner must make certain all the concepts fit appropriately. Thinking through the ethical nature of the strategy or tactic is as important as thinking through the legal and regulatory implications. After all, just because something can be done does not mean it should be done.

For affluent physicians, the Innovation Process operates in the background. Nevertheless, for us, it's perpetual and instrumental in our ability to exceed the expectations of our clients.

The Eight Core Elements of Advanced Planning

In a preceding section we discussed the four interrelated services that constitute advanced planning—wealth enhancement, estate planning, asset-protection planning and charitable giving. We also noted the intellectual aspect of advanced planning—the Innovation Process.

There are further considerations in advanced planning, however, and those of the utmost importance are the criteria that can predict success for affluent-physician clients—the eight core elements of advanced planning. Advanced planning must be:

- Flexible
- Discreet
- Transparent
- Coherent
- Risk sensitive
- Cost-effective
- Complexity sensitive
- Legitimate

These eight elements operate in concert with each other and must be considered in any affluent-physician client situation. In fact, the more seasoned and successful advanced planners working with affluent physicians have developed a high degree of ingrained competency that is a result of continually working with and thinking about these core elements, which we will now examine in greater detail.

Flexible. Advanced planning must be able to change or adapt in order to meet the exigencies of an evolving situation involving an affluent-physician client's circumstances and/or the financial and legal environments. It is inescapable that laws and regulations will be changed, so successful advanced planners are not only flexible and informed, but they also think through a range of advanced planning scenarios that anticipate those changing circumstances and laws.

Discreet. A high degree of discretion is a prerequisite for any advisor working with affluent physicians. Discretion relates to the nature and details of the interpersonal relationship that is established between the advanced planner and affluent physician. Furthermore, though an advanced planner's strategies are legitimate and lawful, a low profile helps avoid any questions or retroactive changes in the rules. Quality advanced planners always presume that every scrap of paper, every formal communication and every conversation could be scrutinized.

Transparent. Although there is no interest or benefit for anyone to advertise the intricacies of an advanced planning strategy, the plan should nonetheless be made as transparent as possible. Without question, advanced planning is not about hiding or laundering monies; it is about leveraging laws and regulations for the benefit of affluent physicians in order to preserve their wealth. Hence, any viable strategy must be open and available to scrutiny by interested parties such as the government.

Coherent. Although the components of advanced planning can be independent of one another—and, indeed, many strategies can be employed as stand-alones—a certain degree of integration should permeate all advanced planning. That is because the strategies carry within them, to varying degrees, the potential to be used for each of the four advanced planning services and as such they have a bearing on each other and on the affluent physician's planning as a whole. Accordingly, advanced planners should maximize any benefits to their clients by first identifying the synergies and then accentuating their value.

Risk Sensitive. Advanced planning runs along a scale from plain-vanilla strategies at one end to the truly esoteric at the other. Although everything is on the proper side of the legal divide, there is clearly a lot of room to be more or less aggressive. Not surprisingly, a solid number of the most cutting-edge, state-of-the-art strategies are more aggressive. It is therefore crucial that affluent-physician clients and their other advisors understand the level of aggressiveness and realize the pros and cons relative to their risk tolerance.

Cost-Effective. Considering the many state-of-the-art strategies at the disposal of advanced planners, there are instances where being on the cutting edge carries too high a price tag for many affluent physicians. Despite the appeal of such strategies, there are nonetheless times when a more pedestrian yet cost-effective solution is sufficient. In sum, advanced planners in conjunction with their affluent-physician clients need to balance the benefits of a course of action with its costs, both financial and psychological.

Complexity Sensitive. A number of affluent physicians want simple and readily understood solutions to their financial and legal issues. Other affluent physicians rely on their professional advisors to sort out the best solutions for them. We advocate that all our clients understand the essence, if not the details, of the strategies we recommend. This makes it our responsibility to communicate with our affluent-physician clients in a way that enables them to make an informed decision. In effect, we will communicate the character of the strategies we advise on a client-by-client basis, ranging from an abecedarian overview to a highly complex flowchart.

Legitimate. Needless to say, any advanced plan should never incorporate strategies that are—or that might be perceived to be—illegal or unethical. Avoiding taxes by skirting the law is absolutely out of the question. Along the same lines, any allegations of fraudulent transfers or any activity that will result in charges of fraud are also out of the question. Considering how much can be accomplished by staying well within the law, it is only excessive greed, ego or sheer stupidity that results in otherwise-legitimate affluent physicians crossing the line. But with so many shades of gray on the domestic front and even a broader spectrum of gray in the international arena, some very legitimate plans can seem questionable even though they are not. However, this is still a far cry from intentionally skirting the law.

Conclusion

Advanced planning is the process through which some of the most essential needs, wants and demands of affluent physicians are met. In this way, advanced planning should be conceptualized as a set of services, as a system for applying these services and as way of creating powerful tax-wise solutions for each and every client.

Advanced planning is composed of four interrelated sets of expertise: wealth enhancement, estate planning, asset-protection planning and charitable giving. For the purposes of this book, our focus is on estate planning and asset protection.

Underlying the effectiveness of advanced planning is the Innovation Process. This methodology results in a steady stream of ideas, some of which end up becoming state-of-the-art strategies. Mover, there are eight core elements of advanced planning that permeate every strategy.

THE VIRTUOUS CYCLE

One erudite expert in the field defined the Virtuous Cycle as an alchemic process where leading-edge financial and legal advisors use wisdom to broker the identification of solutions to problems and deliver strategies that resolve the issues. This is a little verbose, but this definition captures several key elements—advisor wisdom, solutions to problems and the delivery of strategies.

We have found that some affluent physicians, in seeing the results they obtain, often think of the Virtuous Cycle as financial wizardry and tax rocket science. And compared to what many of them have seen from other financial and legal advisors or have read about in trade publications, the strategies employed by competent advanced planners are indeed akin to financial sorcery.

We think of the Virtuous Cycle in two parts. These parts are communicated in the two words chosen for the concept. The Virtue part refers to the ethical process of serving the needs and wants of our affluent-physician clients. The Cycle part refers to the basic sequencing of phases. The Virtuous Cycle is that process whereby advanced planners strive to best serve their affluent-physician clients.

Operationally, the Virtuous Cycle consists of the phases an affluent-physician client would move through in discerning and employing the proper advanced planning strategies. These Virtuous Cycle phases transverse from start to restart and over again. By following the Virtuous Cycle, an affluent physician's goals, objectives and preferences are addressed systematically through advanced planning.

The Phases of the Virtuous Cycle

The Virtuous Cycle is composed of six phases. Although we identify very distinct phases, in the field this is not nearly as clean. Rarely has one of our affluent-physician clients gone through the process smoothly phase by phase. Because of the uniqueness of each and every one of our affluent-physician clients, the Virtuous Cycle is best understood as a conceptual model or a road map. With this caveat in mind, although we will describe the Virtuous Cycle as a sequential process it must be understood as an eminently fluid one. Still, conceptually, the Virtuous Cycle is composed of the following six phases:

- Profile the affluent physician
- Leverage the professional network
- Present recommendations
- Implement
- Deliver results
- Follow-through

It is critical to realize that in all the phases of the Virtuous Cycle, the physicians and his or her other advisors, such as an accountant, are an integral part of the team. As we will see, advanced planning is predicated on teamwork.

Throughout the Virtuous Cycle, the physician's feedback is continuously solicited. Sometimes the feedback solicitation will be a formal component of the process. At other times, the feedback solicitation will be less structured and more informal. At all times, however, we strongly advocate that whenever one of our clients has an opinion, idea or question, that we hear it.

Finally, it should be noted that there is a full menu of names for client planning processes, including the Cycle of Operations, the 4-Quadrant Planning Paradigm[SM] and Financial Framework IV[TM]. What differentiates the Virtuous Cycle is the way that it draws upon research and analysis. Most other models of the planning process are derived exclusively from limited advisor experience. In the development of such models, the personal experiences or techniques of one or several "top" advisors are studied and serve as models for other advisors. By contrast, the Virtuous Cycle was developed both "in the trenches" and in the "statistical laboratory," and it encompasses years of quantitative analysis of the behaviors that elite advisors employ with the exceptionally wealthy. In this way it can be compared to the best-in-class models derived in any industry as a result of benchmarking and quality-process analysis. The Virtuous Cycle has also been validated through literally thousands of cross-sectional interviews.

Profile the Affluent Physician

In order for an advanced planner to apply his or her talents and skills requires a deep understanding of the unique situation of each client. This includes what the client wants to happen as well as what is meaningful to the client. Thus, we work with each of our affluent-physician clients to develop his or her unique profile. The profile is composed of the array of needs, wants, facts, figures, attitudes, perceptions, preferences, social dynamics, thought processes and so forth that inform us what can and should be done.

In the advisory industry there are as many fact finders as there are advisors to the affluent. Financial institutions, law firms and a host of various types of advisors generate a whole range of fact-finder models. We took a close look at most fact finders used in creating a fact pattern with the wealthy and saw that they tended to be skewed. That is, they focused almost exclusively on the assets and financials. Most of them are, however, light in covering what is really important to the affluent.

We distilled the components of the client profile into six categories referred to as the Whole Client Model. In the Whole Client Model, the information we often require is organized in a six-sector framework. What follows are those sectors and the sample information to be garnered:

Goals & Concerns

- What are the physician's personal and professional goals?
- What does the physician feel obligated to do for children, for other family members, for friends, for society or the world at large?

Relationships

- What family-member relationships (spouse, children, brothers/sisters, parents, etc.) are really important to the physician?
- What is his or her religious orientation?

Financials

- What assets does the physician own?
- How are these assets structured?

Advisors

- Who are the other advisors he or she is currently using?
- What role does each advisor play?

Process

- How often would the physician like to meet?
- How does he or she like to "look at" financial information?

Interests

- What charities does the physician currently support?
- What does the physician do in his or her spare time?

Leverage the Professional Network

Socrates maintained that he was an extremely ignorant man. He held this position despite his great knowledge—or more precisely because of it; he knew enough to understand how much he did not know. Advisors should take this lesson to heart. No matter how vast their expertise, the increasingly complicated nature of advanced planning is such that there will be occasions when they are not fully informed on a subject. At these times, it behooves them to turn to specialists.

In particular, because of the often-complicated nature of the financial dealings and personal concerns of affluent physicians, there are many occasions when we turn to niche experts to supplement our expertise. We are strong advocates of leveraging the expertise of specialists, which is why in Part III, "Selected Advanced Planning Wealth-Preservation Strategies," we coauthored each chapter with a world-renowned authority.

Each specialist in our professional network must meet the following criteria:
- *Specific expertise.* Possessing "unique" knowledge is the first screen in selecting the professional as participant in the network. The expertise in question complements our knowledge and skills.
- *Integrity.* High ethical standards are indispensable in all aspects of advanced planning.
- *Professionalism.* In every way, from responsiveness to inquiries to perpetual learning, the network participants must be true professionals.

The participants in our professional network "fill the gaps" in our skill sets and knowledge base. A well-functioning professional network serves to ensure that the advanced planner is always state-of-the-art.

Present Recommendations

With prospective strategies in hand, we now present our recommendations to the affluent-physician client and his or her other advisors. Presenting recommendations is actually a three-step process when looked at carefully.

The first step is a review of the profile with the client. It is imperative that everyone understands the goals, objectives and issues the same way. Although there is a constant soliciting of feedback from the physician, this is the time when that solicitation process is more intently focused and exhaustive.

During the review any meaningful digression from the core premises and assumptions predicated on the information provided by the affluent-physician client must be seen as a red flag. When a red flag goes up, there is an obvious need to circle back to the profiling phase. Red flags can occur when one or more significant alterations in the client's situation and/or preferences have not been detected.

When the affluent-physician client profile is confirmed, the advanced planner proceeds to a discussion of possible strategies to employ—step number two. Based on how this step proceeds, the affluent-physician client is now ready to make decisions, the most important of which are whether to implement a strategy or go back to the drawing board—step number three.

Implement

Often the easiest part of the Virtuous Cycle is implementation. The reason implementation is—or should be—so straightforward is that by this point in the Virtuous Cycle all the hurdles have been identified and approaches to surmounting them have been specified. That does not mean implementation is easy—in many cases, it calls for a tremendous amount of work. However, it is familiar ground and it is something all top advanced planners do extremely well. The key skill sets in implementation are persistence and precision, not the more draining intuition and analysis.

Take for example, the need to obtain life insurance as part of an estate plan. All the decisions concerning what type, how much and how it should be structured have already been made. The next step is a matter of facilitating the underwriting process. This can take many forms, from working with the underwriting department of an insurance company to creating a new life insurance product in conjunction with a reinsurance company. It also means attending to all the other tasks involved with obtaining the policy, including the physical assessment. But, unlike the earlier phase of the Virtuous Cycle, when goals are discussed and strategies weighed, it is a much more mechanical rather than emotional process, and it is therefore less stressful to all involved.

Deliver Results

The delivery of results is a critical point in the Virtuous Cycle because it sets the stage for follow-through, which will ensure that the goals and objectives of the affluent-physician client are in focus and being met.

At this time we:

- *Reconfirm the affluent-physician client profile.* Once again, it is crucial to ensure that the information upon which the advanced plan was developed and implemented is accurate.
- *Make certain the advanced plan achieved the desired results.* It is imperative that the client is getting what he or she expects and is paying for.
- *Revise the action plan as appropriate.* As implementation is often incremental, there are regular opportunities to modify and adjust strategies to keep everything on track.

Follow-Through

Follow-through is crucial because failing to do so will likely result in the affluent physician not being able to continually preserve his or her wealth continually. Follow-through comes in three forms:

- The focused applications of the innovation process
- Client- and/or advisor-driven contact
- Periodic reviews

Focused Applications of the Innovation Process. The affluent-physician client profile is in our data-management system. So, as the Innovation Process proceeds—as new strategies are developed and validated—we are well positioned to bring selected strategies to those clients who would most benefit from them.

Client- and/or Advisor-Driven Contact. There are many times when an affluent-physician client and/or that client's other advisors will reestablish contact with us because of changes in circumstances. Anything that affects the agenda of the client, such as marriages, births and deaths, often prompts a reconnection. When this occurs, there is a need to update the client profile and then proceed through the various phases of the Virtuous Cycle once again.

Periodic Reviews. Due to the nature of advanced planning, it is a given that we will need to meet intermittently with the affluent-physician client and the client's other advisors to ensure everything is going in the right direction, and that all the moving parts of a strategy are working in concert. Although an annual review is the norm in the investment management field, advanced planning reviews are not governed by the calendar but by the strategy employed and the client's preferences.

Conclusion

The Virtuous Cycle is the process whereby the best advanced planners strive to best serve their affluent clients. The Virtuous Cycle structures the interaction between the advanced planner and the affluent physician. It also creates a set of ethical processes for ensuring that the client's needs and interests are optimized at all times.

At the operational level, the Virtuous Cycle consists of six phases that an advanced planner steers an affluent-physician client through, beginning with profiling and fact-finding and ending with follow-through. However, in the hands of experienced advanced planners, the Virtuous Cycle never stops, because it accommodates constantly changing client needs and circumstances. Advanced planning is not static; it is dynamic and ongoing.

Over the Edge

What would a physician do to save $5 million or more in income taxes? What would a physician do to keep his or her wealth from being lost because of a deranged, vicious ex-spouse? What would a physician do to prevent the spouse of a former partner from reclaiming the equity in a very profitable medical practice? Unfortunately, we have seen a good number of successful physicians, under the guidance of their ethically impaired advisors, take substantial risks to shield their personal wealth, even when the associated risks are inappropriate in every respect—let alone being illegal or unethical.

There is a great demand for services that enable taxes to be evaded, just as there is great demand for services that hide assets from litigants or tax-effectively facilitate the transference of ownership interests. And among physicians there are no doubt times when taking such action can be very inviting. Couple these times with a relatively small number of unscrupulous advanced planners and the result is that physicians will end up losers.

Recognizing that a relatively small number of unprincipled advanced planners and their affluent-physician clients will seek to bend or circumvent the law, we regularly uncover a broad variety of approaches that range from legal to questionable to illegal. One example of this is the misuse of trusts.

Misused Trusts

There are many ways for affluent physicians to go "over the edge," including employing abusive trust structures. Abusive trust schemes usually entail the creation of a number of trusts, whether domestic or offshore, to which the client assigns selected assets as well as income. The trusts are vertically layered so that each trust distributes income to the next trust. Bogus expenses are charged against the trust income, thereby reducing the taxable income. At the same time, the illusion of separation and control is created.

Another misuse of trusts is when a physician employs offshore trusts solely as a way to attenuate tax liabilities. Too often, however, offshore trusts are overpromoted as cure-alls by corrupt advanced planners who do not fully understand the strict legal requirements that make the trusts work for affluent physicians. Some of the more common complications include forced heirship rights, direct or indirect control, and inappropriate letters of wishes. Although offshore trusts can be a very potent tool in an advanced planning strategy (see Chapter 8, "Asset-Protection Planning"), they are often wrongly used with promises that are impossible to keep.

The Fine Line of Legality

Moving away from the black zone of clearly illegal acts, we enter the far more complicated and murky gray zone, where the legality of a given strategy is open to interpretation. This is the dominion where an advanced planner's integrity, or lack thereof, becomes readily apparent.

Given the many shades of gray, how does a physician know when a state-of-the-art strategy, especially a relatively new one, crosses the line of legality? How aggressive is too aggressive?

A strategy is too aggressive, for example, if its sole economic benefit is to enable an affluent physician to pay less in taxes or dodge legitimate creditors. In the former case the advisor is engaged in tax evasion for the wealthy; in the latter, the advisor is hiding money and usually involved in fraudulent conveyances.

In interacting with fellow advanced planners and affluent-physician clients, we have seen many strategies that are aggressive to the point of being highly questionable. Tax shelters, in particular, are very detrimental to everyone involved. Still, there is no authoritative definition of abusive tax shelters, which are often obscured behind tax-saving sales pitches. Nevertheless, when the affluent physician engages in a series of transactions solely to mitigate income taxes, there is a problem—a very serious problem.

Clearly, there are a minority of advanced planners and affluent physicians whose moral compasses are encased in lodestone spinning wildly in every direction. It is incumbent on all professional advisors, however, to not employ strategies that are pieced together with the express goal of evading taxes or secluding money, and, above all, to not employ strategies that may compromise their clients. For us, if an affluent-physician client insists on employing such strategies, even after the legal and ethical issues as well as the pitfalls have been pointed out, we will end the relationship.

Why Walk the Fine Line?

So why do some advanced planners and their affluent clients knowingly go over the edge? Why do they take the risks that carry potentially severe consequences? What is the primary justification for being overaggressive?

To address this issue, we examined 118 cases. Each case can be characterized as not being, prima facie, illegal. That is, we are not talking about money laundering for example, but instead considering cases where the strategies employed were overaggressive and proved to be over the edge. The penalties for the affluent clients involved included fines, interest, paying back taxes and in a number of the cases the loss of significant assets as the questionable wealth-protection or wealth-transfer strategies were voided by the courts.

For the advanced planners, there were also severe penalties. Some lost their professional licenses, and an astonishing 109 out of the 118 (92.4 percent) were sued by their affluent clients (Exhibit 5.1), a percentage that should deter any thoughts of going over the edge.

Exhibit 5.1 | Percent of Affluent Clients Who Sued Their Advanced Planners

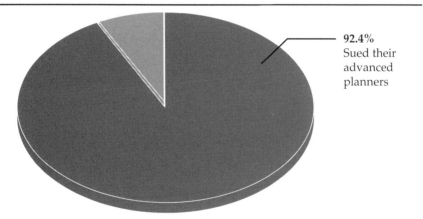

92.4%
Sued their
advanced
planners

N = 118 Cases
Source: Advanced Planning with the Ultra-Affluent (2002)

By coding legal documents and employing a cluster-analytic methodology, we are able to categorize the primary justifications for being overaggressive into three categories that also show the meaningful differences between the motivations of the affluent clients and their advisors (Exhibit 5.2).

Exhibit 5.2 | Primary Justifications

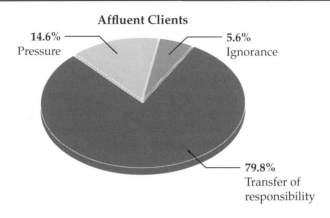

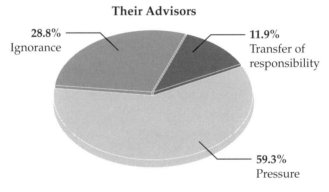

N = 118 Cases
Source: Advanced Planning with the Ultra-Affluent (2002)

Ignorance (a.k.a., the "I didn't know" defense). In this case, affluent clients claimed to have been unaware of what was going on and ignorant of the consequences of their actions. Interestingly, they did not blame their advanced planners for leading them astray. At the same time, more than a quarter of the advanced planners also excused their behavior by claiming ignorance. If they were truly ignorant, it demonstrates the fact that far too many self-proclaimed advanced planners are in over their heads with respect to this field and when they came across an enticing strategy or tactic, they failed to—or elected not to—educate themselves on the possible ramifications and consequences.

Transfer of Responsibility (a.k.a., the "It was his idea" defense). Wealthy clients turn to advanced planners because they want to benefit from the advisors' expertise, and when it comes to advanced planning, those clients are often unable to fully understand and evaluate the recommendations they receive. So it is easy to pass the buck and blame their advanced planners when things go wrong. This was far and away the most common justification adopted by affluent clients, and it is also the reasoning behind their lawsuits. Advanced planners looking to dodge responsibility will in turn sometimes blame other advisors, and, in at least one case we know of, accuse the client of having led them astray.

Pressure (a.k.a., the "I was forced to do it" defense). Some clients claimed that they were compelled to go wrong because of the promise of financial benefits and their financial needs. For advanced planners, financial and competitive pressures were the leading justification for their actions. In order to win business, the advanced planners concluded that they had to be able to provide services that differentiated them and, unfortunately, they sometimes went too far.

The Hidden Justification

The above justifications, based on an analysis of various documents, identify the legal rationales for why some advanced planners and clients are overaggressive. However, based on our working with many successful specialists and affluent clients, we have found a hidden justification for being overaggressive that correlates with both the transfer of responsibility and the pressure justifications: the cost-versus-benefit calculation. In other words, given the amount of money involved, the risk of being caught is deemed worth taking.

Playing the audit lottery, for example, is becoming more attractive to a growing number of the wealthy. At the same time, the amount of time, energy and mental firepower that the government can bring to bear is not equal to the clever ways that some advanced planners can alter and hide assets through a dizzying series of ingenious transactions. As a result, a select portion of affluent physicians and their advanced planners will continue to be overaggressive because they perceive the benefits outweigh the risks.

Factor in the justifications put forth by the affluent and their advisors in their defense and the fact that so many advanced planners are technically in over their heads (see Chapter 6, "Caveat Emptor") and it becomes evident that we will continue to see advanced planners and clients employ strategies that will likely come back to haunt them.

A Personal Note

It is up to advanced planners, through their understanding of the legal consequences and their ethical grounding, to draw the line short of the edge—often way short of the edge. Although it can be ever so enticing and for many advanced planners a process of sophisticated puzzle solving, the absolute need to view all strategies through an ethical lens is a must.

With great regularity affluent physicians come to us so that they can implement strategies they have heard of that, after we take close look, are clearly over the line. Or they are looking for solutions that require using strategies that blatantly cross the line. If these physicians maintain their positions after we have carefully explained why what they want is illegal or highly immoral, we make sure to put considerable distance between them and ourselves. As we noted, because there are so many advanced planning strategies that many physicians can legitimately use to protect their wealth, going over the line—with all the potential financial and personal downside—is just foolish.

Conclusion

Saving money, particularly on taxes, and expanding their wealth is regularly a priority for affluent physicians. So too is making sure their wealth stays their wealth. Given the amount of monies involved and the motivation of physicians as well as their advisors to preserve their wealth, new strategies are constantly being devised. Although some of these strategies are perfectly legal, others are either illegal, unethical, or so clearly conceived to circumvent established laws that they will soon be adjudged illegal.

Advanced planners will scour the landscape for emerging strategies. And although the ability to use such strategies can be enticing, the financial benefits should not entice physicians or advanced planners into crossing ethical or legal boundaries. Moreover, it is the advanced planner's responsibility to draw the line at the edge of innovation rather than take a risk, however measured, that could jeopardize an affluent-physician client's wealth and reputation.

CAVEAT EMPTOR

Advanced planning, as we have started to see, is not the fare of the over-whelming majority of financial and legal advisors. The reverse is the case. Relatively speaking, there are few high-quality advanced planners and fewer still who are attuned to the world of affluent physicians.

To make finding and working with a top-of-the-line advanced planner even more complicated is the fact that in the taxonomy of advanced planning there are subspecialties. Adept advanced planners must not only be able to work with affluent-physician clients through the Virtuous Cycle, but they must also be cognizant of the many strategies that can be utilized and, of extreme importance, be able to leverage a professional network of niche experts.

For affluent physicians to be best positioned to preserve their wealth, irrespective of unanticipated misfortunes and a more inhospitable professional medical environment, the services of high-quality advanced planners are often required. Moreover, physicians need to work with the advanced planners they employ and not simply blindly use suggested strategies. Therefore, an affluent physician needs to select an advanced planner carefully and know how best to work with him or her—the focus of this chapter.

Finding a High-Quality Advanced Planner

There are a variety of ways the wealthy locate all sorts of professionals with whom they then do business. Whether it's for legal services or financial services, the optimal means of finding a topflight professional is through referrals. Affluent physicians tend to turn to someone whose judgment they trust to provide them with an introduction to the type of professional they are seeking.

The very same logic holds for advanced planners. The nature of all high-end services makes referrals a risk-mitigation strategy in selecting a provider. Specifically, we're referring to:

- The intangibility of the offering
- The perceived complexity of the offering
- The desire by physicians to work with "authorities," coupled with a general inability to identify the "authorities"

Intangibility. For most affluent physicians, advanced planning is something of a mystery. The strategies can rarely be "seen or touched" or evaluated directly. There is no way you can do the side-to-side comparison as you might for a stereo system, or road test these services as you would when buying a new car. Thus, it's wise for physicians to turn to referrals from people whose judgment they trust.

Complexity. In our experience, the financial concerns of affluent physicians are important, unique and complicated. Consequently, they will need to find an advanced planner who can address the variety of concerns and issues they face, all with a focus on wealth preservation. Although many so-called advanced planners can talk a good game, few can really deliver. If an affluent physician wants someone who can efficaciously deal with the complexity and particularities of his or her world, he or she will need to get a referral to an advanced planner with a proven track record in this regard.

Reliance on "Authorities." We have yet to meet an affluent physician who did not want to work with an expert—a true authority on developing, crafting and implementing strategies for the wealthy. The best way to find out if an advanced planner is an authority on dealing with wealth preservation for affluent physicians is to get the opinions of other affluent physicians or, better yet, other authorities. What we see is that the significantly wealthy physicians generally turn to people whose opinions they give considerable credence when it comes to selecting advanced planners.

Nearly all of our affluent-physician clients come to us through referrals. From affluent physicians introducing us to their peers, to being called in by professional advisors to address the complex needs of their wealthy physician clients, referrals are the way we find our clients. This is the norm for all advanced planners catering to any segment of the financial elite.

Although affluent physicians may introduce their peers or other professionals will bring in advanced planners they vetted, the affluent physician must still control the selection process. To this end there are a number of guidelines an affluent physician should adhere to in selecting an advanced planner.

Five Criteria for Selecting an Advanced Planner

The competencies of professionals, whether they are physicians or advanced planners, are often difficult to judge effectively. This is even more the case with advanced planners as the quality of some of the strategies provided cannot be truly evaluated until it's too late, if at all.

An asset-protection plan, for instance, can only be determined to work if the physician is in the unfortunate position of being sued. And if the advanced planner did a less-than-competent job, it's too late to correct the situation. Or consider a state-of-the-art estate plan. Will it work as promised? The physician, personally, will never know although his or her heirs will.

What this means is that the affluent physician will often just have to trust the judgment of the advanced planner he or she hired as well as the judgment of his or her other advisors. That does not mean the affluent physician should select an advanced planner without carefully screening him or her. On the contrary, it is the physician's responsibility to do due diligence on the prospective advanced planners he or she might use.

There are five criteria that prove very useful when selecting an advanced planner:

- Criterion #1: Proven integrity
- Criterion #2: Extensive technical expertise
- Criterion #3: Access to niche experts
- Criterion #4: Sensitivity to client needs
- Criterion #5: Experience in working with affluent physicians

By carefully using these criteria as a means to screen prospective advanced planners, affluent physicians will be able to avoid the plethora of financial and legal advisors more than happy to provide them with much less than they are paying for. It's not uncommon for all sorts of con artists and professional incompetents to target affluent physicians. With respect to advanced planning we are dealing with sophisticated legal-based strategies and generally complex financial products that can be very advantageous to preserving wealth. Consequently, it's the bottom-line responsibility of the physician to make sure the person he or she is working with is one of the "best of the best."

Criterion #1 | Proven Integrity

Let us make no mistake about it. Integrity is first on the list of criteria. The veracity of the advanced planner chosen is critical to the affluent physician's ability to safeguard his or her wealth. As patients must trust a physician's judgment, the complexity of advanced planning strategies necessitates the physician trust the advanced planner's judgment.

Although not restricted to advanced planning, we found that more than two-fifths of the affluent physicians (40.4 percent) in our national survey reported being "cheated" at one time or another by a corrupt advisor (Exhibit 6.1). This was more the case for the wealthier physicians (56.8 percent) as they are more likely to be targeted by criminals.

Exhibit 6.1 | "Cheated" by Corrupt Advisors

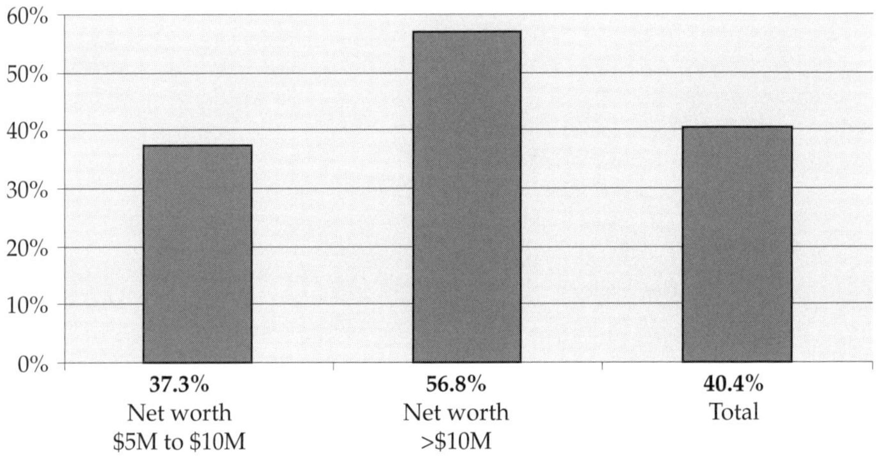

	37.3%	56.8%	40.4%
	Net worth $5M to $10M	Net worth >$10M	Total

N = 941 Affluent Physicians

These physicians mistakenly took the advice of corrupt advisors. They entrusted money to what they now recognize were scam artists. And the result of taking the advice of these shysters was an expensive lesson in life.

One wealth-preservation concern of affluent physicians, for example, that has been ripe for shysters is asset-protection planning. The more blatant examples include promoters hawking offshore solutions such as "unbreakable secret trusts" and "your own bank," to the marketing of pure trusts otherwise known as patriot trusts, contract trusts, final trusts, foreign common law trust organizations and complex trust systems.

A majority of affluent physicians (59.9 percent) have been pitched asset-protection scams (Exhibit 6.2). Once again, the wealthier physicians were more heavily targeted (78.4 percent compared to 56.5 percent). There is no question that being sued for malpractice or the perception of being "rich" is a significant concern and problem (see Chapter 8, "Asset-Protection Planning"). However, there are relatively few professional advisors who are truly competent to deal with wealthy physicians.

Exhibit 6.2 | Were Pitched Asset-Protection Scams

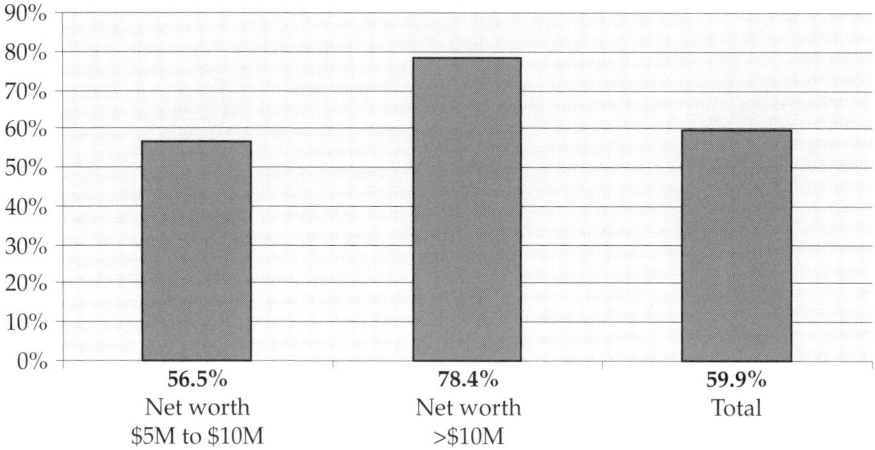

N = 941 Affluent Physicians

Most people believe physicians—all physicians—are wealthy (see Chapter 8, "Asset-Protection Planning"). This, coupled with physicians' very busy schedules and their perceived financial fragility (see Chapter 2, "Sources of Financial Dissatisfaction Among Affluent Physicians") is why physicians tend to be prime targets for corrupt advisors. Consequently, obtaining referrals from peers and trusted advisors such as bankers, investment advisors, lawyers and accountants is our recommended way to select high-quality advisors. Moreover, especially when it comes to "interesting" investments, we will direct affluent physicians to a personal security specialist (see appendix). Very often a little financial-advisor due diligence can produce literally millions of dollars in savings.

As we noted, because of the nature of advanced planning it is usually impossible for someone outside the high end of the business to effectively judge the advice. Therefore, what is very important for physicians is to be able to understand how the advanced planner approaches the business.

An affluent physician, for example, should ask the advanced planner under what conditions he or she would fire a client. As previously noted, we are periodically in situations where affluent physicians ask us to help them do things that are illegal. After explaining the illegality to the physicians, and they do not back off, we fire them.

At other times, the requests are not illegal, but we are moving quickly from the gray to the black. Once again, we detail our position and we will almost invariably recommend a sophisticated but absolutely legal strategy. If the physician prefers his original plan, then that physician is not someone we want to do business with. We strongly believe that there are more than enough ways to help affluent physicians preserve their wealth without having to push the rules to where they are about to break.

Along the same lines, affluent physicians should ask advanced planners what they would *not* do. In effect, the physician is looking to see where the advanced planner draws the line beyond which he or she will not go. How far into the gray area is the advanced planner willing to travel? Although we do make use of a fair number of more aggressive strategies, we are very cautious and make sure all the strategies we use are not going to make our affluent-physicians clients famous in a bad way.

Criterion #2 | Extensive Technical Expertise

As we discussed in Chapter 3, "The Nature of Advanced Planning," bringing the type of extensive technical expertise needed very often requires a team of leading-edge professionals. This need also necessitates criterion number three: access to niche experts. At the same time, all affluent physicians certainly want to work with someone who is talented and very capable.

An advanced planner should have a broad understanding of the various strategies that physicians can use. Furthermore, an advanced planner should have a comprehensive, in-depth understanding of a niche specialty such as how to construct asset-protection plans or how to leverage a captive insurance company. In effect, the best advanced planners have a broad understanding of the panoply of strategies as well as a deep understanding of at least one of the four advanced planning services—wealth enhancement, estate planning, asset-protection planning, or charitable giving.

There are a number of different ways of determining if someone is a technical expert. The referring source is a very good starting point. This is even more the case when another professional advisor introduces the physician to the advanced planner.

Educational attainment and being recognized in the financial and legal industries as an expert is probably one of the better ways to identify truly capable advanced planners. Published works, speaking engagements and the like are signs that other professionals in the field recognize the technical expertise of the advanced planner.

Even among well-intentioned advanced planners there is a clear hierarchy of talent and capabilities. This is the case among professionals who specialize in asset-protection planning, for instance. In a study sponsored by *Trusts & Estates* magazine, we were able to discern that only a small percentage of private-client lawyers who identified themselves as being specialists at asset-protection planning were indeed knowledgeable concerning many of the asset-protection strategies that the wealthy can—very legitimately—bring to bear.

We found that there is a significant gap between private-client lawyers' current competency levels and their ideal skill levels (Exhibit 6.3). Only 16.3 percent of the lawyers surveyed currently rate themselves as authorities on asset-protection strategies and techniques even though they readily position themselves as asset-protection specialists. There are other indications of a low level of expertise. Just 13.2 percent of private-client lawyers say they are very familiar with the Uniform Fraudulent Transfer Act. Moreover, private-client lawyers agree that there is an expertise gap. Overall, 73.6 percent agree that they need to become more knowledgeable about asset-protection strategies.

Exhibit 6.3 | Delivering Asset-Protection Expertise

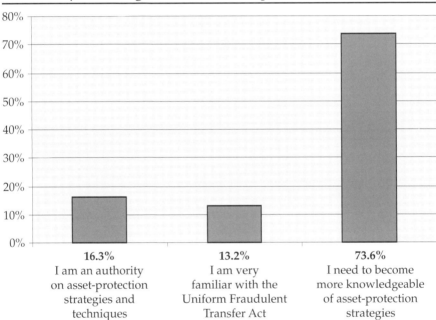

16.3%	13.2%	73.6%
I am an authority on asset-protection strategies and techniques	I am very familiar with the Uniform Fraudulent Transfer Act	I need to become more knowledgeable of asset-protection strategies

N = 227 Self-Identified Asset-Protection Lawyers

Another indication that many private-client lawyers need to enhance their asset-protection expertise is that a meaningful number of them are unfamiliar with some of the more common strategies in the field (Exhibit 6.4). Although most are comfortable with such strategies such as corporate structures, outright gifts to family members and limited liability companies, far fewer felt they were experts in areas such as offshore self-settled trusts, life insurance and equity stripping.

Exhibit 6.4 | Familiar With Specific Asset-Protection Strategies and Techniques

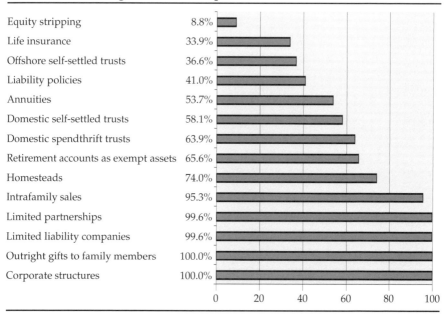

Equity stripping	8.8%
Life insurance	33.9%
Offshore self-settled trusts	36.6%
Liability policies	41.0%
Annuities	53.7%
Domestic self-settled trusts	58.1%
Domestic spendthrift trusts	63.9%
Retirement accounts as exempt assets	65.6%
Homesteads	74.0%
Intrafamily sales	95.3%
Limited partnerships	99.6%
Limited liability companies	99.6%
Outright gifts to family members	100.0%
Corporate structures	100.0%

N = 227 Self-Identified Asset-Protection Lawyers

This survey indicates that significant percentages of private-client lawyers do not feel completely prepared to offer asset-protection planning at the level of professionalism appropriate for affluent physicians or any wealthy individual for that matter. These private-client lawyers feel they need more expertise in the area in order to deliver the quality of service they are accustomed to giving.

When it comes to advanced planning, it's not just in the area of asset protection that so many self-proclaimed experts prove to be anything but. With respect to estate planning strategies, there are many well-intentioned, self-proclaimed experts who fail to recognize all the risks associated with their recommendations or are able to provide high-quality legal documents.

Premium financing is a way to use borrowed monies to purchase life insurance. It is a very valid approach—under the right conditions. Increasingly we see more and more affluent physicians who financed their life insurance and have run into big problems. What was sold to them as "free" life insurance will end up costing them a great deal of money. What is happening is that the advisors who sold them the life insurance, including the lawyers who signed off on the strategy, did not understand the strategy very well and ended up selling something inappropriate for the physician.

For the affluent physicians who have been referred to us with this problem, we have been able to *work out* the strategy. In most cases, we are able to eliminate or severely mitigate the current or forthcoming balloon expenses. And in a number of situations we have been able to provide the affluent physician with a viable solution. This enables them to achieve the same results they were initially looking for without the downside complications.

An affluent physician must never forget that we are talking about his or her wealth. Consequently, it's that physician's responsibility—his or her obligation—to make sure that the advanced planner he or she is working with is one of the "best of the best."

Criterion #3 | Access to Niche Experts

No matter how technically adept an advanced planner is, he or she cannot know all the nuances about all the various strategies that can be used to protect a physician's wealth. No one is an advanced planning polymath. Anyone making this claim is lying and should be avoided—refer to criterion number one: proven integrity.

For advanced planners, the answer is not in possessing omnipotent advanced planning knowledge. True advanced planning polymaths are exceedingly rare when the moon is blue and Aquarius is in the House of Sagittarius. This being the case, the answer is for advanced planners to have access to an array of high-quality niche experts, specialists who can work hand-in-hand with them and their affluent-physician clients.

It's often a wise move for an affluent physician to have a discussion with the advanced planner about his or her professional network of specialists. Who are they? Why were they chosen? How does everyone work together? How are the niche experts compensated? Not only does this enable the affluent physician to gauge the capabilities of the advanced planner better, it also enables the physician to gain some insight on the way the advanced planner works.

Criterion #4 | Sensitivity to Client Needs

It's fair to say that the vast majority of affluent physicians do not know all the different strategies that exist or how they can be used to promote optimal wealth preservation. Moreover, it is not the physician's job to go to his or her advanced planner and explain what strategies to use. It's the advanced planner's job to bring innovative ideas to the physician's attention!

The advanced planner an affluent physician wants to work with is one who spends the time to really understand what the physician wants to accomplish, spends the time to understand all of the physician's doubts and anxieties, and then is *always* thinking of ways to be responsive. This is why the Virtuous Cycle is central to advanced planning and why the Whole Client Model is essential (see Chapter 4, "The Virtuous Cycle").

In Part III, "Selected Advanced Planning Wealth-Preservation Strategies," we will provide brief descriptions of a number of strategies that can be used by affluent physicians personally or within their practices to preserve their personal wealth. It's important to realize that we're not advocating any of these strategies—that would be a disservice. Only when we truly understand our physician clients as unique individuals, and only by understanding the way their practices are structured and are operating can we make meaningful recommendations.

Criterion #5 | Experience in Working with Affluent Physicians and Their Practices

The backgrounds, the stresses of the profession, and the lifestyles of affluent physicians are unique (see Chapter 2, "Sources of Financial Dissatisfaction Among Affluent Physicians"). They are not the same, for instance, as those of families who own manufacturing companies or corporate executives of Fortune 500 companies.

It is an irrefutable fact that physicians work in a very distinctive profession. Although advanced planning is applicable to all manner of the wealthy, the world of the affluent physician and his or her practice provides idiosyncratic opportunities for wealth preservation. It is therefore smart for affluent physicians to work with high-quality advanced planners who are attuned to their world—the world of medical professionals.

For all the research and for all the education into the various advanced planning strategies, experience in working with affluent physicians has provided us insights that cannot be obtained in any other way. These insights are crucial to understanding how the various strategies can be most effectively employed. And, as we just noted, there are some strategies, such as leveraging captive insurance companies to mitigate malpractice premiums and increase the physician's private wealth, that are unique to medical practices.

Affluent physicians want to work with professionals who truly understand their world. Hence, an advanced planner who has extensive experience working with affluent physicians will be the optimal choice.

How to Work With an Advanced Planner

Finding a top-notch advanced planner is not enough. The affluent physician still has to work with him or her to get the most out of the relationship. It's therefore very important that affluent physicians have an overview understanding of the way the advanced planner works and the rationale behind the recommendations he or she presents.

Working with a high-quality advanced planner is an education. At the end, affluent physicians should not expect to be proficient in the field, but they should understand what they are "buying." We have found that far too many affluent physicians neglect to take the time to understand what they are agreeing to, with adverse consequences. The following four guidelines can help in this regard:

- Guideline #1: The advanced planner should explain the Virtuous Cycle.
- Guideline #2: The advanced planner should explain the alternative ways an affluent physician can preserve wealth.
- Guideline #3: The affluent physician should not be restricted concerning with whom he or she can discuss a recommended strategy.
- Guideline #4: The advanced planner should explain how the various recommended strategies interact.

Guideline #1: The advanced planner should explain the Virtuous Cycle. Although different advanced planners might have their own variations on the Virtuous Cycle, basically the steps we detailed are key. Hence, it is important that affluent physicians know what to expect from their advanced planners, and the best way to do this is to make sure the advanced planners walk them through the Virtuous Cycle or some variation of it.

Guideline #2: The advanced planner should explain the alternative ways an affluent physician can preserve wealth. In advanced planning there is rarely a single strategy that can meet the needs and wants of the client. On the contrary, there are many possible strategies resulting in sometimes different, sometimes similar outcomes. The affluent physician, in conjunction with the advanced planner and other advisors, needs to select the strategy that is best for him or her. Therefore, it's essential for the affluent physician to understand the trade-offs with respect to the various strategies.

Guideline #3: The affluent physician should not be restricted concerning with whom he or she can discuss a recommended strategy. As we discussed, it's not uncommon for advanced planners and their physician clients to go over the line. One way these unscrupulous promoters seek to mitigate their risk of getting caught is by having their clients sign nondisclosure or confidentiality agreements. In fact, these promoters tend to require the physician's other professional advisors to sign such agreements as well.

Based on our research, about a third (35.4 percent) of the affluent physicians were asked to sign a nondisclosure agreement (Exhibit 6.5). And this was more common among wealthier physicians (54.7 percent compared to 31.8 percent). The reason for this difference is that many of the questionable strategies hiding behind nondisclosure agreements are only applicable for people with greater wealth.

Exhibit 6.5 | Asked to Sign a Nondisclosure Agreement

| | 31.8%
Net worth
$5M to $10M | 54.7%
Net worth
>$10M | 35.4%
Total |

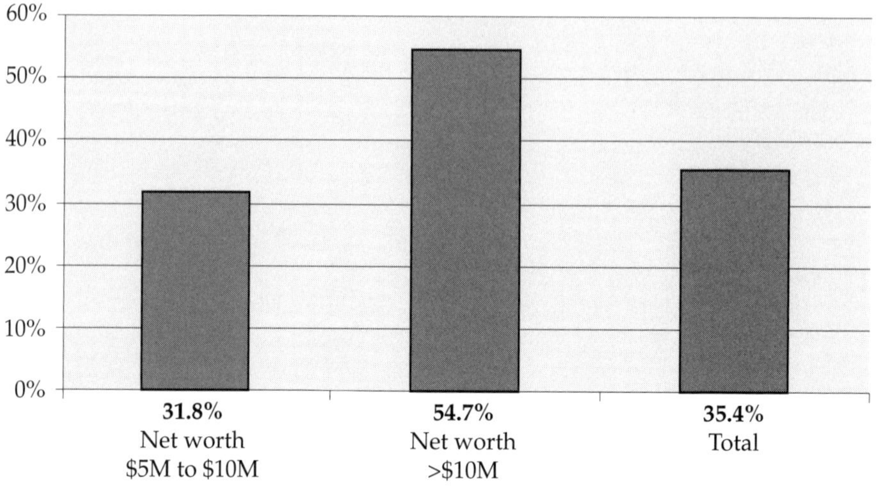

N = 941 Affluent Physicians

Affluent physicians should not sign nondisclosure agreements. As we explained in Chapter 3, "The Nature of Advanced Planning," one of the eight core elements is transparency. Furthermore, the physician's other professional advisors should never sign such agreements as they likely conflict with their fiduciary responsibilities to the physician.

Guideline #4: The advanced planner should explain how the various recommended strategies interact. For us, advanced planning is about providing the very best strategies to physicians so that they can maximize their wealth. That means it's important to understand how all the pieces work together as there are synergies that can result. This often entails working closely with the affluent physician's other professional advisors.

A Personal Note

We regularly meet and work with affluent physicians who are more than happy to abrogate all responsibility for their financial well-being. They are more than content in turning everything over to us. The problem is that we will not work *for* affluent physicians, but we will work *with* them and their other professional advisors.

Because of the characteristics of advanced planning, the type of physician we will work with is *intelligent* and *informed*. By and large, we do not have to concern ourselves with intelligent. At the same time, we see it is as our responsibility to provide the information so that our affluent-physician clients can make informed decisions.

Conclusion

To maximize a physician's personal wealth by leveraging the tax code and regulations as well as employing financial products in often-unique ways will require the assistance of a high-quality advanced planner. Although there are many "professionals" who hold themselves out as experts in advanced planning, the advice of most of them will probably prove more deleterious then beneficial.

In the end, the most important decision affluent physicians can make in their desire to preserve their wealth is going to be whom to turn to for advanced planning expertise. Focusing on referrals either from peers or other advisors and following the five criteria will likely result in finding a high-quality advanced planner.

At the same time, affluent physicians are integral to the success their own advanced planning strategies. This requires their involvement even if it's only from up high.

PART
III

SELECTED
ADVANCED
WEALTH-
PRESERVATION
STRATEGIES

ADVANCED ESTATE PLANNING

With Edward A. Renn

Cautionary Tale #1 | There's Plenty of Time to Plan Later

Things had gone very well for Dr. Gibson. He entered the field of cardiology in an era when new medical treatments for people with advanced heart disease seemed to come out on a monthly basis, and he always managed to stay on the leading edge of advanced care. Dr. Gibson was a success, both professionally and financially. By the time he was 62 he had amassed a portfolio in excess of $15 million, about half of which was in an IRA. He had a $2 million apartment in New York City and a $1 million beach house in Westhampton. His lifestyle, however, had always remained relatively modest; he and his wife were spending about $350,000 a year. Dr. Gibson's first marriage was not a success, but he and his second wife had been happily married for over nine years. His children were grown and doing nicely for themselves. He was happy and was finally beginning to look forward to retirement.

Dr. Gibson had an estate plan. It left $1 million to his wife, just as their prenuptial agreement required. He wanted to leave the rest of his property to his children, and we convinced him to leave it in trust, rather than giving it to his children outright. The trusts took full advantage of his exemption from the generation-skipping transfer (GST) tax and kept the assets protected in case any of the children got divorced or had creditor problems. Unfortunately, his advisors could never convince Dr. Gibson to do any lifetime planning. "I'll get to it eventually," he always said.

About eight weeks after we had our last meeting with a seemingly healthy Dr. Gibson, he was dead. He died of a rare blood ailment. By the time he was diagnosed it was too late. His family paid over $7.5 million in estate taxes. The children received the $7.5 million IRA and the New York apartment, but the IRA is still subject to state and federal income tax when they withdraw the money. Taking into account the unpaid income tax, the children were getting only about $6.5 million of their father's $18 million estate!

Cautionary Tale #2 | The Illiquid Estate

I remember when Dr. Goldstein and his wife first walked into my office. I had been working with his accountant for years, and his accountant had been trying to convince him to see me for almost that long. With the death of his brother a few months before, Dr. Goldstein finally decided it was time to talk.

By the end of our first meeting, I knew we had a problem. Dr. Goldstein was 70 years old and was about to retire from the practice of medicine. He tended to invest conservatively. He told me he had tried investing heavily in the stock market but it gave him too much stress for too little return; after all, he lived comfortably on his conservative investments and he could sleep at night without worrying about the stock market. As a result, Dr. Goldstein had a $3 million IRA that was invested entirely in bonds and CDs. The couple also owned a $3 million house in Fairfield County, Connecticut, a $1 million house in Florida, and some commercial real estate worth about $10 million.

Dr. Goldstein had also been a lifelong patron of modern artists and had amassed an art collection that he insured for $10 million. Although the art collection contained works from a host of artists, ten painters were responsible for over 80 percent of the collection's value.

Dr. Goldstein had an estate worth over $27 million, and the only liquid assets were the assets in the IRA. I estimated the estate tax due upon his wife's death would be over $11 million, and if the IRA was used to pay estate taxes it would be subject to immediate income tax, making it worth less than $2 million to a beneficiary. Dr. Goldstein didn't think he had a problem: "You can sell the house, some property or some art," he said.

"The estate tax is due nine months after your death and there is no guarantee we can find a buyer for a $3 million house in that time," I explained. "We might be forced to sell it for much less than fair market value. And if we sell even half of your art collection we would flood the market and drive down prices," I added. Clearly, the Goldsteins had a serious liquidity problem.

Cautionary Tale #3 | *The Foreign Spouse*

When Dr. Swift died, he left behind his wife, an English citizen he met as a student in London over forty years ago. He also left behind their two children, both of whom held only U.S. citizenship after surrendering their U.K. citizenship when each turned 18. He also left an estate worth $20 million. Before he died, Dr. Swift had an estate plan prepared by the same firm he had been using for 20 years in relation to his business dealings. They had drafted leases and various contracts for him and had represented him in various lawsuits. They were good lawyers and he trusted them.

The lawyers prepared their standard estate plan, which consisted of a will and a revocable trust. Under this plan, two trusts were set up when he died. The first, a "credit-shelter trust," was designed to hold the amount he was entitled to pass without estate tax by using his "unified credit." The second was a marital trust that was intended to qualify for the marital deduction. The lawyers told Dr. Swift and his wife that by using this plan there would be no estate tax due at the first of their deaths.

Dr. Swift and his wife trusted their children, so the plan called for all trust property to be distributed outright in equal shares if the children were at least 35 years old when the surviving parent died. The share for any child who was under 35 would be held in trust for him or her until the child turned 35, and then it would be distributed.

Despite Dr. Swift's best efforts, his daughter, Julie, became a lawyer. She was actually quite a successful lawyer and she was my client. When Dr. Swift died, Julie asked me to review her father's estate plan to find out if her inheritance would be exposed to her creditors. Her firm was sued for malpractice from time to time.

The estate plan had a number of problems. First, the lawyer who drafted the estate plan had used a Qualified Terminable Interest Property (QTIP) trust, which he expected to qualify for the marital deduction to the estate tax. This would have worked if Mrs. Swift had been a U.S. citizen. Because she was not, the lawyer should have drafted a Qualified Domestic Trust (QDOT). This mistake caused $18.5 million of the $20 million estate to be subject to estate tax, triggering an unnecessary tax of almost $8.7 million!

Second, the credit-shelter trust, which would hold $1.5 million, directed the trustee to make distributions of principal to Mrs. Swift and their children for their "health, education, maintenance and support." This is what estate planners refer to as an "ascertainable standard," because a court could ascertain how much a beneficiary was "supposed" to receive from the trust, making the beneficiary's right to distributions enforceable by court order even if the trustee refuses to make distributions.

Unfortunately, if Julie's law firm loses a malpractice case, the plaintiff may be able to get a court to order a distribution from the trust for Julie's "maintenance and support" and then seize those funds. Julie may get some protection from the fact that the trust was also supposed to benefit her mother and brother; this might make a court reluctant to order large distributions to Julie alone. However, because Julie was 36 and her brother Michael was 33 when Dr. Swift died, their creditor-protection situation would get even worse when Mrs. Swift also passed away. Upon her death, Julie and Michael will receive their inheritance outright, exposing it fully to their respective creditors.

Dr. Swift's son, Michael, was not a professional facing the risk of a malpractice suit, so he thought the outright distribution would be fine. After all, he was responsible with money and getting the property outright was just simpler. He changed his mind on his 35th birthday when he received divorce papers from his wife. Her lawyer wanted to include the trust property as part of the divorce estate because it was only a matter of time before he received the distribution.

At some level, nearly everyone is a candidate for estate planning. Estate planning is for people who:

- Want to decide how their assets will be distributed at their deaths instead of relying on the wisdom of the state
- Want to decide how and when heirs receive their inheritance instead of depending on state laws
- Want to ensure that the maximum amount possible is transferred to their loved ones while paying the least amount of tax

At the very least, everyone with anything in the way of assets should engage in basic estate planning. On the other hand, not everyone—including those people who are by many standards wealthy—are candidates for advanced estate planning. Just what is advanced estate planning?

> **Advanced estate planning is the process of using strategies to legally structure the future disposition of current and projected assets.**

Advanced estate planning resolves some of the most challenging legal issues faced by affluent physicians. It makes use of sophisticated strategies that are most appropriate for a thin slice of the population.

Before we discuss some of the strategies that constitute advanced estate planning, let's consider how affluent physicians are addressing this matter today.

Affluent Physicians and Estate Planning

It's not a surprise that nearly all the affluent physicians we surveyed say that they are concerned about having properly provided for loved ones when they die (Exhibit 7.1). The real issue is what steps they have taken on behalf of their loved ones.

Exhibit 7.1 | Concerned For the Well-Being of Loved Ones

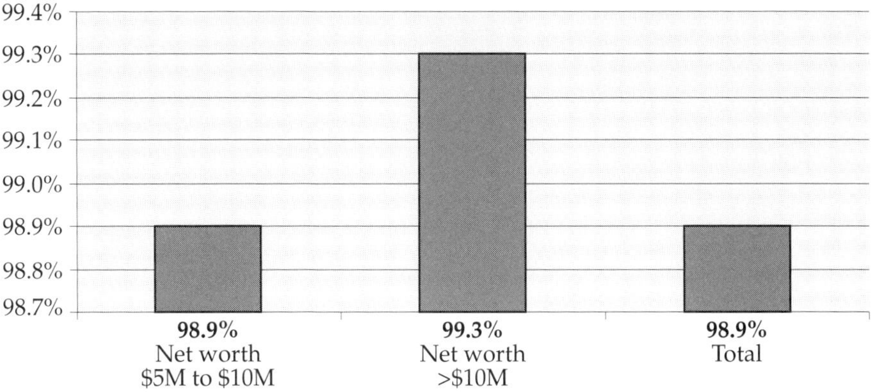

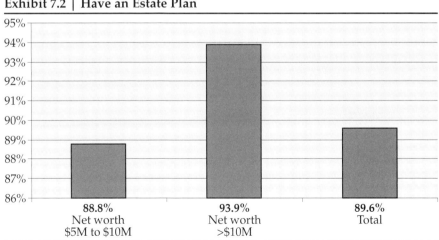

N = 941 Affluent Physicians

Nine out of 10 affluent physicians (89.6 percent) have an estate plan (Exhibit 7.2). Slightly more of the wealthier physicians have an estate plan (93.9 percent) compared to the less wealthy physicians (88.8 percent). What this also means is that 98 affluent physicians do not have an estate plan, and we wanted to know why.

Exhibit 7.2 | Have an Estate Plan

N = 941 Affluent Physicians

We employed a factor-analysis technique to derive the principal motivations *not* to have an estate plan (Exhibit 7.3). For many (42.9 percent), the topic is a very difficult one to deal with. The emotional strain and stress proves too arduous, and avoidance proves an easier course of action.

A similar number of affluent physicians (41.8 percent) cite their schedules as the reason they have not focused on estate planning. Faced with hectic and demanding practices and numerous family obligations, they know it would be a good idea, but they just cannot seem to find the opening in their calendars.

Another 10.2 percent report that they do not have a need for an estate plan. These affluent physicians generally point to two reasons. One is that everything will just go to their spouses. Although this may very well be the case, it can be shortsighted. The second reason they give is that they are not wealthy enough. When people tend to equate estate planning with wealth, they tend to focus on estate taxes. No matter what happens with estate taxes, if a physician wants to direct how his or her assets are distributed, then an estate plan is warranted.

Finally, 5.1 percent said that estate planning was too expensive. Without question, estate planning can be expensive, but the benefits to the family can greatly exceed the cost. Therefore, for us, it's a requirement to deliver value that is a multiple of the fees charged.

Exhibit 7.3 | Why No Estate Plan

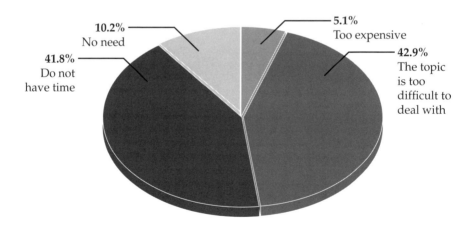

N = 98 Affluent Physicians

Returning to those affluent physicians with estate plans, although it is impossible to evaluate directly the quality of the plans we can use proxies. To begin with, we asked about the age of their estate plans (Exhibit 7.4).

For a majority of affluent physicians (52.4 percent) their estate plans are more than six years old. For another 34.8 percent, their estate plans are between three and six years old. Only a sixth of the physicians (12.8 percent) have estate plans less than three years old. Furthermore, a small percentage of the wealthier physicians had older estate plans than the less affluent physicians.

Exhibit 7.4 | Age of Estate Plans

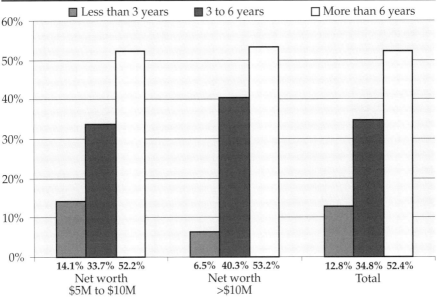

| ■ Less than 3 years | ■ 3 to 6 years | ☐ More than 6 years |

| 14.1% 33.7% 52.2% | 6.5% 40.3% 53.2% | 12.8% 34.8% 52.4% |
| Net worth $5M to $10M | Net worth >$10M | Total |

N = 843 Affluent Physicians

Why is the age of an estate plan a proxy of its quality? No matter how well conceived and implemented an estate plan is, after a few years it's out of date because politicians and the Treasury are perpetually tinkering with the tax code.

It's not only modifications to the tax code that date an estate plan; changes in a client's life have the same affect. For example, 87.8 percent of the affluent physicians are wealthier now than when they did their estate plan (Exhibit 7.5). This is proportionately more common among the more affluent physicians (94.2 percent compared to 86.5 percent). In a substantial number of cases, the physicians are wealthier by multiples.

Exhibit 7.5 | Wealthier Since the Estate Plan

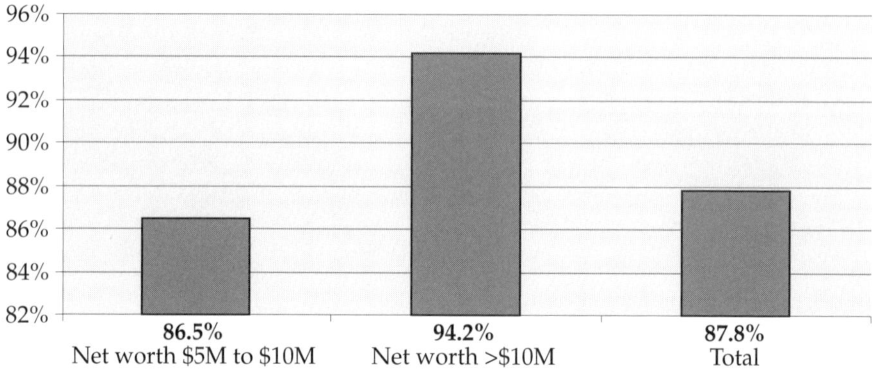

| 86.5% | 94.2% | 87.8% |
| Net worth $5M to $10M | Net worth >$10M | Total |

N = 843 Affluent Physicians

Another indication that most of these estate plans are stale is that about three quarters (76.4 percent) of affluent physicians have experienced a major life-changing event since their estate plans were written (Exhibit 7.6). Life-changing events can seriously reduce the effectiveness of an estate plan. Life-changing events include birth of a child or grandchild, a divorce, a death in the family, a marriage and so forth.

Exhibit 7.6 | Experienced a Life-Changing Event Since the Estate Plan

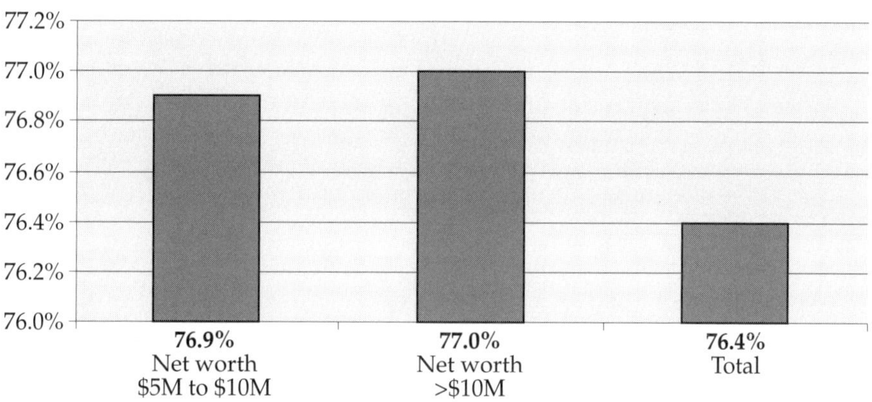

| 76.9% | 77.0% | 76.4% |
| Net worth $5M to $10M | Net worth >$10M | Total |

N = 843 Affluent Physicians

In sum, although most affluent physicians do indeed have estate plans, it's highly likely that they are out of date. Whether it's from changes in the tax code or from life-changing events, these old estate plans are unlikely to accomplish the current goals and objectives of affluent physicians.

Compounding the problem is that most estate plans for the wealthy were not at the cutting edge—or even in the neighborhood—when they were written. Consequently, by having estate plants that were behind the curve when they were written, and are now stale as well, many affluent physicians are missing the opportunity to maximize their wealth.

Transfer Taxes

In order to discuss some of the advanced planning wealth-preservation strategies mentioned below, we must briefly review the basics of the transfer tax system. There are three transfer taxes at the federal level:

- *The Gift Tax.* The gift tax is a tax imposed on the transfer of property during a person's life. The person making the gift has the primary obligation to pay the tax. In general, an individual may give as much property as he or she wants to his or her spouse without incurring any gift tax, so long as his or her spouse is a U.S. citizen. This is because the law allows an unlimited marital deduction for the amount passing directly to a U.S. spouse. Gifts to a trust for the benefit of your U.S. spouse may also qualify for the marital deduction if they are in a proper form, typically a QTIP trust, and reported on a timely filed gift-tax return.
- *The Estate Tax.* The estate tax is imposed on the transfer of property after the owner's death. Once again, you can leave an unlimited amount of property to your U.S. spouse without incurring any tax. If you wish to leave property in trust rather than leaving it to your spouse outright, the trust must meet certain requirements, but in general, it's still possible to claim a marital deduction.
- *The GST Tax.* The GST tax is designed to ensure that a transfer tax is imposed at each generation as wealth is inherited, even if a gift "skips" a generation.

The following summarizes the most important points to remember about the transfer taxes we touched on:

Gift Tax

- Generally, an affluent physician can give an unlimited amount of property to his or her U.S. spouse without incurring gift tax.
- An affluent physician may make taxable gifts of up to $1 million of property during his or her lifetime to anyone without incurring federal gift tax.
- An affluent physician can generally give up to $11,000 per year to anyone without it counting as a taxable gift.
- Payment of tuition or medical expenses directly to the provider does not count against the $11,000 annual limit.
- An affluent physician can give up to $117,000 a year to a non-U.S. spouse without making a federally taxable gift.

Estate Tax

- Generally, an affluent physician can leave an unlimited amount of property to his or her U.S. spouse without incurring estate tax.
- When leaving property to a non-U.S. spouse, an affluent physician must use a QDOT or he or she cannot claim a marital deduction.
- There is a credit that allows affluent physicians to pass up to $1.5 million without paying estate tax, but most taxable gifts made during their lives will use up a part of this credit.

GST Tax

- The tax is imposed on transfers to grandchildren or younger family members.
- The tax may also be imposed when property is transferred to a trust for the benefit of grandchildren or where property is distributed from a trust to a grandchild unless the trust is made exempt from the GST tax.
- There is an annual exclusion from the GST tax that is similar to the gift tax annual exclusion.
- There is a $1.5 million exemption from the GST tax that can be used during life or at death.
- GST exemption is automatically used for outright gifts, but gifts in trust may require the filing of a gift or estate tax return.

Collectively we refer to these taxes as "transfer taxes" because they are taxes imposed on the privilege of transferring wealth. The tax rates for these transfer taxes reach as high as 47 percent. In fact, the GST tax is a flat tax at the highest estate tax rate—currently 47 percent. (The top tax rate in 2005 is 47 percent, but this rate is scheduled to decrease to 46 percent in 2006 and 45 percent in 2007.) In addition, many states impose their own transfer taxes, which raise the overall tax burden, but for simplicity, and because it represents the biggest tax bite, we will focus on the federal system.

Selected Estate Planning Strategies

There is a multitude of estate planning strategies that affluent physicians can employ. In this chapter we will briefly consider:

- Revocable trusts
- Life insurance planning
- Qualified personal residence trusts
- Grantor-retained annuity trusts
- Sale to a grantor trust
- Family limited partnerships and limited liability companies
- Charitable lead annuity trusts

These particular wealth-transfer strategies are often appropriate for affluent physicians. There are many other possible strategies that can be employed as well as the various permutations we get when combining strategies. Let's now examine each of these strategies in some detail.

Revocable Trusts. Why talk about revocable trusts in a discussion on advanced estate planning? Revocable trusts are fundamental documents, but not all revocable trusts are created equal. The revocable trusts that a lot of estate planning lawyers draft are simply not appropriate for high-net-worth individuals such as affluent physicians. The three most common flaws observed in revocable trusts are:

1. They do not keep wealth in trust long enough.
2. They do not have the right distribution standard.
3. They provide inadequate control over the trustee.

Many people, like Dr. Swift and his wife, have trusts that terminate in favor of their children once the children turn 35. Affluent physicians should generally keep property in trust as long as possible. There are two basic reasons for this: creditor protection and tax savings. If properly drafted, a trust protects property from a child's creditors, including in most cases, potential divorcing spouses. Whether it's a lawsuit or a divorce, trusts keep family money safe. Furthermore, a long-term trust takes advantage of the physician's GST exemption. When affluent physicians distribute property to their children, it's included in the children's taxable estates. If the affluent physicians were to place the property in GST-exempt trusts that are designed to benefit their children during life but not be taxable in any child's estate, then any dollar the children do not need during life can be passed to grandchildren free of transfer tax, potentially saving millions!

Many trusts authorize distributions for a person's "health, education, maintenance and support." An "absolute-discretion" standard is a much better choice because it offers far more flexibility and superior creditor protection. If a child wanted money for something other than health, education, maintenance and support, the trustee cannot make the distribution even if he or she thinks it is a good idea! There is usually no good reason to restrict a trustee this way. On the other hand, if a child files bankruptcy or is in the midst of a divorce, a health, education, maintenance and support standard creates the possibility of a judge ordering a distribution for "maintenance or support," which may then be seized by a creditor or divorcing spouse. An absolute-discretion standard eliminates this possibility, providing superior creditor protection.

As for control, we often see a series of trustees named. There are a lot of reasons there are problems with this approach, not the least of which is that 20 years from now everyone named will be retired and they may not want to deal with the responsibility of being trustee. Worse yet, we sometimes see a bank named, and the bank has the ability to name its own successor. Commercial trustees often do a great job, but this structure simply gives them too much power. Someone should always have the ability to evaluate the job the trustee is doing and to change the trustee if necessary. One option is to give the children the ability to remove the trustee and name a successor. This will make them feel like they have as much control over the property as if they owned it directly, but they will have all the benefits trust planning provides. Another option is to have a "protector," whose sole power is to change the trustee. The point is for the affluent physician to give as much thought to who will control the trust as to who will get money from it. We advocate a system that is flexible and provides some checks and balances.

Life Insurance Planning. For physicians facing liquidity problems, such as Dr. Goldstein and his wife, life insurance can provide a simple and efficient solution. If they purchased a second-to-die life insurance policy with a $12 million death benefit, their liquidity problem goes away. Whether buying such a policy is feasible depends on their health and the size of the resulting premiums.

It is also important that the insurance policy be owned by an irrevocable life insurance trust. Otherwise, the full value of the death benefit would be included in the Goldstein's taxable estates and half the death benefit would be lost to estate taxes! Assets held in a properly structured irrevocable trust would not be included in an affluent physician's taxable estate.

When Dr. Goldstein and his wife have both passed on, the insurance trust can use the cash from the insurance to purchase assets from the estate or revocable trust. The estate gets cash it needs to pay the estate tax, and the insurance trust would hold the purchased assets for the benefit of Dr. Goldstein's family while also protecting the trust assets from creditors and further transfer taxes.

The issue with life insurance in a trust is how to pay the premiums in a tax-efficient manner. If Dr. Goldstein pays the premiums directly, the payment will be treated as a gift to the insurance trust and use a portion of his $1 million gift-tax exemption. This is not efficient. The solution to this problem is often provided by using "Crummey" powers or withdrawal rights. Crummey powers are named after the family who first litigated their use. In general, they work as follows:

1. Dr. Goldstein transfers money to the insurance trust.
2. Each of the trust beneficiaries (in this case, Dr. Goldstein's two children and three grandchildren) are given the right to withdraw up to the annual exclusion amount (currently $11,000) for a limited period of time, say 30 days. This right to withdraw makes the gift to the trust qualify for the annual exclusion to the gift tax.
3. If Dr. Goldstein's wife also plans to contribute to the trust, or elects to "split" her husband's gifts on their gift-tax returns, we can provide

for a withdrawal right that will use her annual exclusions too, raising the per-beneficiary withdrawal right to a maximum of $22,000. For the Goldstein family, this results in a total tax-free contribution to the trust of $110,000 a year. Because these transfers use the Goldstein's annual exclusions, none of their $1 million gift-tax credit equivalents are used up.

4. To ensure that these transfers are respected, the individuals with the right to withdrawal will be given written notice of that power.

5. To the extent the withdrawal powers are not exercised, the trust will use the cash contribution to pay insurance premiums.

6. Although the transfers to the trust will qualify for the gift-tax annual exclusion, they will not qualify for the annual exclusion to the generation-skipping tax. To make the trust exempt from the generation-skipping tax, Dr. Goldstein and his wife may need to file gift-tax returns allocating a portion of their GST exemptions to the trust. The total GST exemption allocation will be equal to the amount contributed to the trust. Allocating GST exemptions in this manner can provide tremendous leverage because by allocating the premiums as they are paid, the entire trust, including the full value of the insurance death benefit, becomes exempt from GST tax.

Sometimes the amount of money that can be transferred to an insurance trust through the use of annual exclusion/Crummey gifts is not adequate to pay the required premiums. There are a variety of techniques that can help resolve this problem.

One solution is premium financing. In essence, a third-party lender loans the insurance trust the amount it needs to pay the annual premium. In exchange, the lender takes a security interest in the death benefit (and in some cases other assets as well).

The insurance policy can be structured with a fixed death benefit or with a death benefit that increases in proportion to the amount of debt incurred to pay the premiums. In the case of Dr. and Mrs. Goldstein, they could consider an insurance policy with a net death benefit of $12 million, so that if the premiums were $200,000 a year, in year three the gross death benefit would be $12.6 million, providing the trust with enough assets to pay back the $600,000 loan and leave a net death benefit of $12 million, which could then be used to pay estate taxes.

Traditionally, the insured was expected to pay the interest on the loan annually. In other words, the insured would continue to make some gifts to the trust, using annual exclusion gifts where possible, and these gifts would provide the funds necessary to pay interest on the loan, but the principal amount would increase annually as premiums were paid. For some affluent physicians, even getting enough money into the trust to pay the annual interest can be problematic. Fortunately, there are some insurance products available today in which the insured does not even have to pay the interest!

Premium financing can be very useful for some clients because it allows time to use other estate planning techniques, like a Grantor Retained Annuity Trust (GRAT) or a sale to a grantor trust (discussed below), to build funds outside the client's estate that can later be used to pay insurance premiums. For example, an affluent physician who makes a large sale to a grantor trust or who places a large amount of property in a GRAT will receive a very large note or annuity payments back over the next few years. The trusts involved will have relatively poor excess cash flow for a few years while the annuity or note payments are being made, but the physician will still have a fairly high potential estate-tax burden. Financed life insurance allows the family to put in place insurance now, but pay for it later. Ten years from now there will be assets in trust providing a large positive cash flow, more than enough to pay the insurance premiums.

Qualified Personal Residence Trust. Using a Qualified Personal Residence Trust (QPRT), affluent physicians may pass their primary residence or a vacation home to the younger generation in a tax-efficient manner. This strategy takes advantage of the time value of money and works particularly well in times of high interest rates. For example, Dr. Gibson has a beach house in Westhampton. If he established a QPRT, it would work as follows:

1. Dr. Gibson would deed the house into the QPRT. Under the terms of the trust, Dr. Gibson would retain the right to live in the house for a specified term—15 years, for example.

2. Dr. Gibson would make a gift of the right to his house after 15 years. The value of that gift is the present value of $1 million to be received in 15 years. Each month the IRS publishes interest rates that can be used to value future gifts. Recently the rates have been fairly low, around 4.6 percent. Using that rate, the value of Dr. Gibson's gift would be approximately $500,000. If the interest rate were higher, say 6.6 percent, the gift would only be about $380,000. The term of the trust also affects the amount of the gift.

3. In this case Dr. Gibson would be giving the remainder away instead of having someone purchase it, but the valuation analysis is basically the same. The size of the gift is based on both the length of Dr. Gibson's retained interest and the interest rates in effect at the time. Whatever the size of the gift, it is a gift that will take effect in the future and so cannot be offset by annual exclusions. In other words, this gift would use up a portion of Dr. Gibson's unified credit.

4. If Dr. Gibson dies during the term of the QPRT, the full value of the house would be included in his estate. However, if Dr. Gibson survives the 15-year term, no part of the property would be included in his estate. If the property appreciates at an average of 4 percent a year, it will be worth $1.8 million. So, by using somewhere between $380,000

and $500,000 of the $1 million he can give without paying gift tax, Dr. Gibson would have moved $1.8 million out of his estate. The more valuable the property becomes, the greater the benefit from doing this planning.

The question then becomes how can Dr. Gibson be able to continue using his Westhampton home at the end of the 15-year period. His spouse would be a beneficiary of the QPRT, and Dr. Gibson can continue using the property as her guest. If Dr. Gibson gets divorced or his wife dies, he would have to pay rent to use the house. Ironically, rent payments are advantageous from an estate planning perspective because they transfer additional property from Dr. Gibson to his family (or a trust for their benefit), shrinking his estate and increasing the assets that are protected from creditors.

The Grantor Retained Annuity Trust. A Grantor Retained Annuity Trust (GRAT) is a trust into which the grantor gifts property and retains the right to receive an annuity payment for a period of years. The value of the gift associated with forming a GRAT is the value of the remainder interest, just as with a QPRT. Think of it this way: what is the right to a pool of assets worth if someone must first wait for some number of years, during which a fixed amount will be returned to the person who set up the fund? If the period was very long or the annual payment very high, the remainder would not be worth very much at all.

Selecting an appropriate payout rate and term are very important. The risk that the grantor does not survive the term of the GRAT is a serious one because, as with the QPRT, the entire value of the trust may be taxed as part of the grantor's estate if he or she dies prematurely.

Often an affluent physician will choose to "zero out" a GRAT. In other words, using the IRS's calculation tables, the value of the annuity is so high that as far as the IRS is concerned, there will be no property left in the trust when the annuity stream ends, and consequently, the value of the gift is zero.

Unlike the QPRT, this technique works best when interest rates are low. This is because the lower the interest rate is the easier it is for the experienced investor to outperform. As long as the assets in the GRAT appreciate faster than the IRS's assumed rate of return, there will, in fact, be assets left in the GRAT when it terminates even if the GRAT has been "zeroed out." This is essentially a tax-free gift of property.

What is more, because the GRAT is a grantor trust, the grantor pays any income tax due on the investments of the trust. As a result, if the current interest rate is 4.6 percent, the GRAT only needs to have its investments grow faster than 4.6 percent on a **gross basis**, in order for this technique to be effective.

Although the concept of the GRAT is specifically set out in IRS regulations, the ways in which they can be structured do vary. Three variations in particular bear mentioning:

- Rolling GRATs
- Series GRATs
- Increasing GRATs

The idea of rolling GRATs is that the affluent physician creates successive short-term GRATs. In other words, an affluent physician sets up a GRAT with a two-year term and a very high payout. When that two year GRAT expires, the physician puts the annuity payments received into another two-year GRAT and so on and so on. The goal is to capture all of the "upside" in the market inside the trust. For example, if an affluent physician placed $1 million into a two-year GRAT and the trust annually appreciates at 15 percent, $172,000 would remain in the trust at the end of the two-year term. Obviously, a 15 percent annual rate of return over a two-year period means that the physician's investment performed above the market's historical average, but it is not unusual that some investments beat the market in any given two-year period. If during the next two-year period the investment's rate of return was 5 percent, then all of the trust property would be returned to the physician, the grantor. When we compare two two-year GRATs versus a single four-year GRAT it's clear that this structure is effective at capturing the upside of volatile investments.

In a series GRAT plan, an affluent physician establishes several GRATs of various lengths and funds all of them when the plan begins. For example, the physician might create GRATs of three years, seven years and 15 years. Once again, the goal is to hedge against market fluctuations by providing various periods of time over which we hope funds will appreciate more than had the physician simply picked a single term and funded it to a larger degree.

Certain types of investments, especially illiquid or hard-to-value assets, present difficulties when placed in short-term GRATs. One alternative for "startup" investments is to create a GRAT in which the initial annuity is small and increases gradually. It's possible to increase the dollar amount of an annuity payment by up to 20 percent a year. This is generally advantageous because the goal is to leave money in the GRAT and growing for as long a period of time as possible. It's also highly useful if the early years of an investment are expected to be less profitable than those that follow.

Sale to a Grantor Trust. In many ways selling an asset to a grantor trust is similar to establishing a GRAT. The sale transaction is generally structured as a sale in return for an installment note, so in either case the trust gets the grantor's asset, and the grantor gets a series of payments back over a term of years. In many situations however, the grantor trust sale will produce even better transfer-tax savings.

A grantor trust is a trust that is treated as if all of its assets were owned by its grantor, so that for income tax purposes it is indistinct from its grantor. The affluent physician who sets up one of these trusts must report all the income and deductions associated with the assets in the trust on his or her personal income tax return. Such a trust, however, need not be included in his or her estate.

There are many types of grantor trusts—in fact a GRAT is one type of grantor trust. In this context a grantor trust is a trust in which the grantor retains no beneficial interest—no right to distributions—and as a result the trust can be outside of the grantor's taxable estate immediately. The grantor retains some minor administrative right—a unilateral right to buy the trust's assets by giving the trustee assets of an equivalent value, for example—and because of that becomes responsible for all of the trust's taxes, even though he has no right to distributions. Why is this a good thing? Well, it means that the assets of the trust grow on a tax-free basis, because the grantor is picking up its tax tab. The payment of taxes on the trust's income and gains is effectively a transfer tax-free gift to the trust, but that's not the only thing that's good about it. When a trust is a grantor trust, the grantor can sell assets to it without triggering an immediate capital gains tax—and that's about to become very useful.

The affluent physician forms a grantor trust and sells assets to the trust in exchange for a promissory note. The physician does not recognize any gain on the sale because a person cannot sell something to himself or herself, and for income tax purposes the IRS will treat a grantor trust as just another bank account that belongs to the physician. The trust will repay the note using either the income generated by the asset transferred into it, or by cannibalizing the principal of the asset in the trust. The note will generally be at the lowest interest rate that can be charged without the foregoing of interest constituting a gift, because we want the trust to pay as little as possible back to the physician. This rate is published monthly by the IRS and is referred to as the applicable federal rate.

In most instances the affluent physician should make a small taxable gift to the trust before entering into the sale. This prevents the IRS from arguing the transaction was a sham because no one would sell property to someone (or a trust) with no ability to repay. As a rule of thumb most estate planners tend to gift 10 percent of the total value being transferred.

As an example, assume an affluent physician gifts $500,000 to a grantor trust and sells $4.5 million in stocks and bonds to the trust in exchange for a nine-year self-amortizing note at a time when the applicable federal rate is 4 percent. The total transfer is $5 million. If the assets appreciate at 10 percent per year, at the end of nine years the affluent physician will have received a total of $5,446,966 in note payments and there will still be $3,571,188 in the trust. Without this planning there would be an additional $3.5 million in his or her taxable estate. Through this planning the affluent physician saved $1.75 million of estate taxes. With proper planning, the entire amount is exempt from the GST tax, meaning it can pass to his or her grandchildren without incurring a second level of taxation at 47 percent. If we look ahead another 10 years using the same investment assumptions, the trust will have grown to about $9.25 million—all of which will pass without further transfer taxes.

Family Limited Partnerships and Limited Liability Companies. As efficient as a sale to a grantor trust is, it's possible to add even more leverage to the transaction by using a Family Limited Partnership (FLP) or Limited Liability Company (LLC). A FLP is simply a limited partnership owned by members of a single family or trusts for the benefit of that family. A FLP has two types of ownership: the general partnership interest and the limited partnership interest. A general partner controls the daily operation of the partnership and is personally liable for any debts of the partnership. A limited partner is prohibited from participating in the management of the partnership and is not personally liable for partnership debts. Similarly, a LLC may be structured with voting and nonvoting interests. Although in general no member will share liability for the LLC's debts, nonvoting members will be prevented from having a say in most LLC management decisions.

The sale to the grantor trust must be for "fair market value." The gift-tax system defines fair market value as what a hypothetical willing buyer would pay to a hypothetical willing seller, both having full knowledge of all relevant facts and neither being under any compulsion to act. Under this definition, a limited partnership interest or a nonvoting LLC interest is not very valuable. Compared to the pro-rata value of the underlying property, a discount should be taken for the lack of control a limited partner has and the absence of a ready market for the transfer of such an interest.

For example, if an FLP owns 100 shares of XYZ Company, the owner of a one percent limited partnership interest in the FLP should not be treated as if he owns one share of XYZ Company. After all, he or she has no say in whether to keep or sell the XYZ shares, no access to any dividends XYZ Company might make, and it is extremely unlikely that anyone who wanted to buy XYZ shares would buy his or her limited partnership interest instead of trying to acquire the XYZ shares directly. In short, a "willing buyer" would not pay that much. The actual discount varies, but appraisers generally report anywhere from 30 percent to 50 percent, depending on the nature of the assets and certain other factors.

If instead of transferring $5 million of equities, as we did in the last example, we transferred a 99 percent limited partnership interest in a limited partnership that owned $5 million in equities, the result would be a little different. Assuming a 40 percent discount, the 10 percent gift to the grantor trust (in this case a 99 percent limited partnership interest) would only be worth $297,000. The sale price would not be $4.5 million, it would be $2,673,000. As a result, at the end of 9 years the affluent physician would have been paid only $3.25 million and the trust would retain assets worth $6.8 million! By adding the FLP, over twice as much property was retained in the trust and over twice as much estate tax was avoided.

Charitable Lead Annuity Trust. In our experience, many affluent physicians are charitably inclined. If physicians give cash or stock to their favorite causes, they get an income-tax deduction. It's simple and cheap, but it misses one of the best estate planning opportunities available, the Charitable Lead Annuity Trust (CLAT).

A CLAT operates very much like the GRAT we previously discussed, and like a GRAT it is possible to zero out a CLAT. As with the GRAT, the affluent physician creates a trust and transfers property to it, but the CLAT pays an annuity to a charity of the physician's choice for the fixed term. The identity of the charity can be fixed in the document, or the physician can give the trustee discretion to choose different charities each year. It is also possible to divide the annuity payment among a variety of charities.

When the annuity term ends, any property left in the trust is available to the noncharitable beneficiaries—such as the physician's children. Just as with the GRAT, the value of the gift is the actuarial value of the remainder interest—the value of the right to receive whatever is left after the term is over and all the annuity payments are made. In the case of a zeroed-out CLAT, the IRS tables indicate nothing will remain, but if the trust appreciation exceeds the assumed rate of return, there will in fact be assets left and they pass gift tax-free to the physician's heirs. As with a GRAT, it is possible for the annuity payment to increase annually, and this can add even more leverage to the transaction.

For example, if an affluent physician funds a zeroed-out 15-year CLAT with $1 million when the IRS's interest rate is 4.6 percent and we assume the annuity increases by 20 percent a year while the assets appreciate at 10 percent a year, the IRS believes there will be nothing left at the end of the 15 year term, but there will actually be $1.6 million. That is a tax-free gift of $1.6 million for doing exactly what the physician was already prepared to do—make a generous gift to charity. If the CLAT paid a level annuity instead of increasing by 20 percent a year, only $1.2 million would be left, but the charity would receive a steady stream of cash.

Affluent physicians have a choice when setting up a CLAT. They can receive an immediate income tax deduction for the value of the annuity, but to do that the trust will have to be a grantor trust. In other words, the physician receives an income tax deduction today, but will pay the income tax on the trust's income for years to come. If the physician does not want to pay those taxes, he or she will not get an income tax deduction today. Instead, the CLAT will receive an income tax deduction each year as it makes the annuity payment.

Conclusion

Estate planning saves taxes—often millions of dollars in taxes. It preserves assets in case your loved ones are ever sued or suffer through a divorce. Properly done, an estate plan can be more flexible than direct ownership, while providing these tax and asset-protection benefits for generations to come. For affluent physicians, the opportunity costs of failing to take advantage of the leverage available through lifetime gifting and life insurance cannot be overstated.

The field of advanced estate planning is populated with many strategies, ranging from the relatively basic to the remarkably complex. It is also populated with advisors, few of whom are able to offer the experience and creativity required to meet the unique needs of affluent physicians as they proceed through the estate planning process. As we start integrating various planning strategies with asset-protection planning (see Chapter 8, "Asset-Protection Planning"), the selection of a proper advisor becomes ever more critical.

Asset-Protection Planning

With Jonathan E. Gopman

Cautionary Tale #1 | The Pain of Going Bare

Dr. Marcus, a well-known OBGYN, practiced in a large metropolitan area for over 25 years. He built a highly successful practice, and during his career he accumulated a sizable net worth by taking a significant portion of his income and making some shrewd investments.

In the last five years of his practice Dr. Marcus was sued three times. Most of the physicians and lawyers practicing in the area would refer to these cases as nuisance suits. Nonetheless, a nuisance was deemed an expensive proposition to defend by his malpractice carrier. Thus, in each instance, even though Dr. Marcus' counsel believed his client had a strong defense that would succeed at trial, the insurance company's counsel elected to settle each case for what it believed to be nominal sums ranging from $25,000 to $40,000. After the third case, Dr. Marcus' annual malpractice premium more than tripled to almost half of his annual salary. Rather than continue to pay the exorbitant cost of insurance coverage (which could mean a drastic downgrade in life-style), Dr. Marcus elected to go bare.

After Dr. Marcus dropped his malpractice coverage, he was sued again because one of his patients gave birth to a severely handicapped baby. Most all of the experts in the community agreed that Dr. Marcus conducted himself in an appropriate manner during the birth of this baby and in treating his patient. Nevertheless, the jury rendered a verdict in favor of the plaintiff. Most experts in the community believe Dr. Marcus lost this case because the jury felt tremendous compassion for the plaintiff's situation, believing that someone had to pay for the complications that developed during the birthing process. Apparently a "wealthy physician" was the best possible candidate.

Cautionary Tale #2 | Even When Patients Do Not Listen

A plastic surgeon did a breast-enlargement procedure on a patient. Unfortunately, the patient experienced some minor post-operation complications. Still, such complications were normal problems that can occur following this type of procedure.

The patient was anxious and consulted with the surgeon, who made a number of recommendations. All the recommendations were commonly accepted practice, however, the woman failed to follow any of the physician's recommendations to deal with the problem.

By not following any of the physician's medical recommendations, the situation became more deleterious. As more serious problems occurred, the patient sued the physician for malpractice. To garner support for her case, the woman arranged for a local television station to do an expose on the physician.

Public opinion was not in the physician's favor, which adversely effected the jury pool. The nightmare got worse when the physician could not get the venue changed for the trial. The conclusion was that the physician lost the case and the patient was awarded a multimillion dollar settlement.

Cautionary Tale #3 | Accepted Medical Practice Is Not the Issue

Dr. Williams, an ophthalmologist, performed a procedure on a patient on a Friday. Over the following three-day weekend, the patient experienced postprocedure complications. After telephonic consultation with the patient during the long weekend, Dr. Williams recommended that the patient consult a certain physician at the beginning of the following week.

In making this recommendation, Dr. Williams was following standard practice in the local medical community when these types of complications occur. In other words, any other eye surgeon would have made the same recommendation and not treated this problem as being particularly serious.

Regrettably, the patient developed complications with her vision in the eye in which Dr. Williams performed the procedure, and she claimed the physician's failure to address the problem immediately was a proximate cause to these problems. The patient would have been unable to find any local ophthalmologist who would have done anything differently. Nonetheless, Dr. Williams was sued for several hundreds of thousands of dollars.

Although it is a field of legal planning in its own right, asset-protection planning is a derivative of other types of legal planning. Specific courses are not taught as part of the law school curriculum nor do there appear to be any case books that solely examine the topic of asset-protection planning. As noted, high-quality asset-protection planning is a function of combining expertise from other areas of legal planning. Asset-protection planning is also a risk management process. A high-quality asset-protection plan will leverage current laws to provide an affluent physician with a viable defense for his or her assets in case the physician is confronted with an *unjust* claim by a party who potentially seeks to separate the physician from his or her wealth. In a nutshell:

> **Asset-protection planning is the process of employing legally acceptable concepts and strategies to ensure a person's wealth is not unjustly taken from him or her.**

Bear in mind that when we are involved in asset-protection planning, our objective is to protect the wealth of our clients from *unjust* claims. With the litigation lottery and similar structural malfunctions permeating our society, coupled with the general perception that all physicians are wealthy, asset-protection planning is a wise move for most—if not all—affluent physicians.

In some respects the blatant process of asset-protection planning may work against physicians. When we practice asset-protection planning, it is derivative to economically or legally viable planning. In our case, we are practicing income tax planning and/or estate planning and/or practicing succession planning. Furthermore, when we engage in these forms of planning, we are sensitive to the vulnerabilities our affluent-physician clients have with respect to potential future lawsuits and how this could affect their wealth. Consequently, when we engage in these various forms of legal planning we often simultaneously are protecting our clients' wealth from potential creditors.

Many transactions and structures employed that protect the wealth of affluent physicians from creditors should make economic sense, with asset-protection planning being derivative to these other forms of legal planning. Thus, an attorney can explain to a judge or jury the rationale for these actions based on their economic logic.

The objectives of asset-protection planning are really quite simple:

- *First, it is intended to mitigate the possibility of being sued by motivating a creditor to settle.* In effect, a creditor and his or her attorneys will recognize the situation for what it is and a lawsuit will be avoided. The result is that the physician would likely settle for significantly less than the amount the creditor is attempting to obtain.
- *Second, in the case of a lawsuit, the objective is to minimize or even eliminate the financial effect of a judgment against the physician.* Although a creditor may have prevailed in the lawsuit, the financial burden is greatly mitigated. Many of the physician's assets are simply legitimately not available to satisfy the judgment.

Asset-protection planning is wise legal planning in preparation for the possibility of someone seeking to abscond with an affluent physician's wealth by exploiting the legal system. Hence, it is a form of *prelitigation planning*.

In our experience, we find that the best asset-protection plans are never even tested in court. The preferred course is to avoid litigation. The idea is that after reviewing the way assets have been structured, creditors and litigants conclude that going to court would be too costly and difficult, so they choose to settle.

Thus, asset-protection planning is about being able to stand up in court and justify the way affluent physicians organize their wealth and the manner in which they transfer assets into various legal structures such as trusts, partnerships and corporate entities. Whenever we are dealing with litigation or the possibility of litigation, the key is in the rationale. The advanced planner must take the facts, which may include the logic for the actions taken by a physician, and be able to present such facts in a way that would resonate with a judge or jury. This rationale must convince the court to leave the physician with his or her wealth intact because:

- The physician was morally right in his or her actions.
- The advanced planning strategies implemented were justifiable and appropriate, and that such strategies were economically or legally sound and reasonable given the physician's personal, professional and financial situation.

As noted, asset-protection planning is not about employing structures to protect assets *per se*. In general, judges and juries tend to look down on wealthy and successful people trying to avoid paying their debts, except for in the case of bankruptcy, and then we are quickly not dealing with wealthy people anymore. In contrast, where asset-protection planning is part of a holistic approach and strongly intertwined with other forms of legal planning such as estate planning, we regularly have a viable and court-sanctioned way to employ legal structures as well as the means of transferring assets to such structures that protect wealth.

Let us now consider some more of the findings from our survey of affluent physicians.

Affluent Physicians and Asset-Protection Planning

Many physicians think of or are introduced to asset-protection planning with respect to malpractice lawsuits. Still, about a quarter of affluent physicians (28.5 percent) have been sued for malpractice (Exhibit 8.1). This was more the case with wealthier physicians (36.7 percent) than the less affluent ones (26.8 percent), and it had less to do with specialization as it did with the perceived wealth of the physician by the litigants—a point we will return to shortly.

Exhibit 8.1 | Been Sued For Malpractice

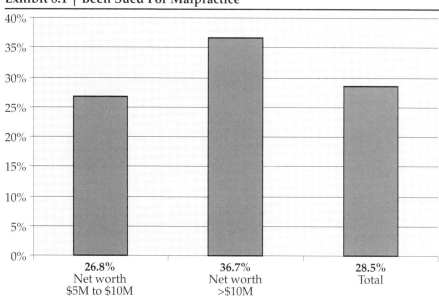

N = 941 Affluent Physicians

More telling is that 71.6 percent of affluent physicians are concerned about being sued for malpractice (Exhibit 8.2). And this time there is not much of a difference between the wealthier and less wealthy physicians (74.1 percent compared to 71.2 percent). So, in general, affluent physicians are concerned about being dragged into a malpractice lawsuit.

Exhibit 8.2 | Concerned About Being Sued For Malpractice

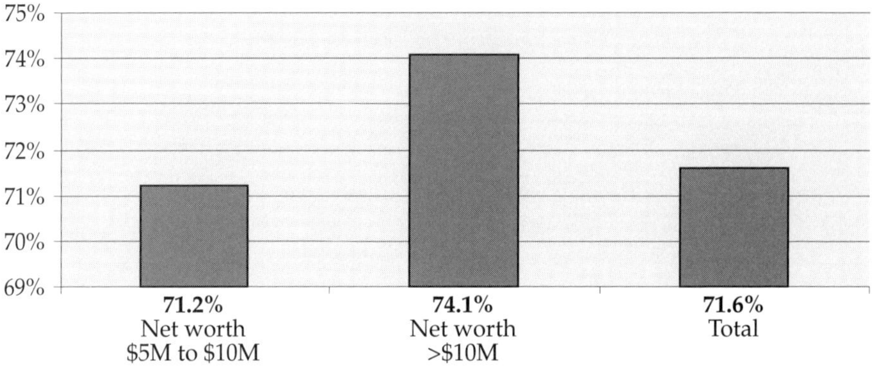

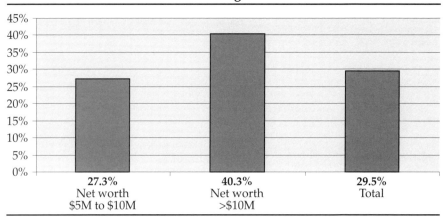

75%
74%
73%
72%
71%
70%
69%
71.2%
Net worth
$5M to $10M
74.1%
Net worth
>$10M
71.6%
Total

N = 941 Affluent Physicians

As we saw in Chapter 2, "Sources of Financial Dissatisfaction Among Affluent Physicians," 82 percent foresee the liability situation getting worse. And few affluent physicians (8.5 percent) are counting on meaningful tort reform rectifying the situation.

Although malpractice lawsuits can be psychologically and monetarily painful, such suits rarely result in financial ruin for physicians. On the other hand, an unjust lawsuit going against them or a messy divorce can decimate years of wealth creation. Overall, 29.5 percent of affluent physicians have been involved in such situations (Exhibit 8.3). This was proportionately more the case among wealthy physicians (40.3 percent compared to 27.3 percent).

Exhibit 8.3 | Been Involved in Unjust Lawsuits and/or Divorce Proceedings

45%
40%
35%
30%
25%
20%
15%
10%
5%
0%
27.3%
Net worth
$5M to $10M
40.3%
Net worth
>$10M
29.5%
Total

N = 941 Affluent Physicians

We also found that affluent physicians understand the consequences of such situations, as 86.6 percent of them are concerned about being involved in an unjust lawsuit or a divorce proceeding (Exhibit 8.4). Again, proportionately more of the wealthier physicians were concerned (92.8 percent compared to 58.4 percent), as they have more to lose.

Exhibit 8.4 | Concerned About Being Involved in Unjust Lawsuits and/or Divorce Proceedings

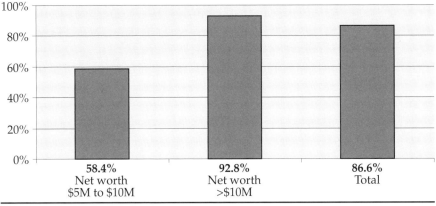

N = 941 Affluent Physicians

In working with affluent physicians, we often find a vague yet powerful fear of non-malpractice lawsuits. The general perception is that a jury will see a physician as wealthy and able to afford the loss easily.

To get a better understanding of this "fear of being seen as wealthy," we randomly surveyed 1,889 individuals with annual incomes of $50,000 or more who did not have physicians in their immediate families. The individuals' average income equaled $81,200 per year and their median income equaled $68,400 per year. Bear in mind that the median income in the country is a hair over $43,000. Evidently, these individuals are not wealthy, however, they do make more than the average American. What we found was that the average person has a warped view of the annual salaries of physicians (Exhibit 8.5).

About half (49.4 percent) believe that the average physician's annual salary is between $300,000 and $600,000. A little more than a quarter of those surveyed (26.6 percent) believe the average physician's annual salary is between $600,000 and $1 million. An eighth (12.3 percent) place the average physician's annual salary at $1 million or more. Only 11.7 percent stated that the average physician annual salary is less than $300,000. With the pervasive perception that all physicians are rich, what physician would like to be judged by six or 12 of these individuals? What physician would want them to determine the appropriateness of a financial settlement?

Exhibit 8.5 | All Physicians Are "Rich"

Average physician's salary	
Less than $300,000	11.7%
$300,000 to $600,000	49.4%
$600,001 to $1 million	26.6%
Over $1 million	12.3%

N = 1,889 Individuals with Annual Incomes of $50,000 or more

Physicians, especially affluent physicians, justifiably tend to see themselves as targets because we live in a litigious society. This deleterious situation is compounded by the fact that the general public tends to think of physicians—nearly all physicians—as being quite well-to-do. This moves the ball into the physician's court. If a physician wants to protect his or her wealth from litigants as well as aberrant ex-spouses and the like, then he or she must take action—and that action entails establishing an asset-protection plan.

Although the logic for establishing an asset-protection plan is rather strong, only 31.1 percent of the affluent physicians we surveyed have done so (Exhibit 8.6). Asset-protection plans were proportionately more common among the wealthier physicians (39.6 percent compared to 29.4 percent).

Exhibit 8.6 | Have an Asset-Protection Plan

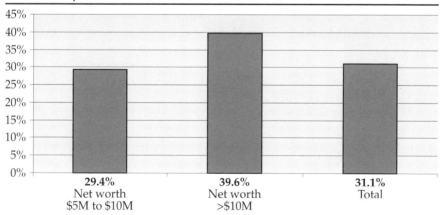

N = 941 Affluent Physicians

As with our analysis of the affluent physicians who have no current estate plans, we used factor analysis to discern the <u>principal motivation</u> for not having an asset-protection plan. Many physicians are quite dubious of promoters hawking asset-protection planning—and rightfully so. In Chapter 5, "Over the Edge," we saw that 59.9 percent of affluent physicians were pitched asset-protection scams. So, although asset-protection planning makes sense and affluent physicians are looking for ways to shield assets legally from litigants and ex-spouses and the like, nearly half the affluent physicians (48.0 percent) report they do not have an asset-protection plan, because they do not know whom to trust (Exhibit 8.7).

A similar percentage (36.3 percent) said they just do not have the time. As with estate planning, these physicians are so time starved that, even when they deem it important, there just is not the opportunity to establish an asset-protection plan. Another 8.8 percent said there was no need for such a plan. A few physicians (3.6 percent) see asset-protection planning as illegal or unethical. Last, 3.3 percent think that it would be too expensive for them.

Exhibit 8.7 | Why No Asset-Protection Plan

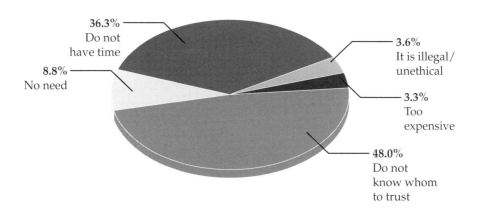

N = 679 Affluent Physicians

Although many affluent physicians have strong reservations about creating their own asset-protection plans, the research clearly indicates receptivity on their part to a powerfully perceived need. As we noted, it's wise for affluent physicians to consider asset-protection planning seriously, and most would forcefully agree.

Let us now consider some of the asset-protection planning strategies that are appropriate for affluent physicians.

Selected Asset-Protection Planning Strategies

As with estate planning, there is a plethora of asset-protection strategies available to affluent physicians. We will briefly consider the following:

- Using state law exemptions
- Forms of ownership
- Use of business entities to hold property
- Restructuring the medical practice
- Asset-protection trusts
- Gifting assets
- Structuring gifts and inheritance to a physician

Using State Law Exemptions. Where does the affluent physician live? Perhaps this is the most important question of the planning process. Why is residency so critical? Depending upon where the physician lives, the law may provide the physician with one or more "exemptions" that allow him or her to protect wealth from the claims of a creditor.

Exemptions differ from state to state, however, many states provide residents (including physicians) with exemptions for a portion or all of the cash value of life insurance, an annuity contract, a retirement plan, a residence, disability insurance, college savings plans and wage income. The amount of wealth protected by a particular exemption will depend on state law as will the form of ownership required to claim the benefit of an exemption.

Take a Florida resident for example. The state of Florida offers a panoply of generous exemptions ranging from wealth protection for the entire cash value of life insurance policies, retirement plans, annuities and an individual's equity in a personal residence. Nevertheless, to claim the exemption for the cash value of a life insurance policy, the physician must be the insured under the policy. Thus, for instance, the exemption will not apply where the physician claiming the exemption is the spouse of the insured. Furthermore, although a Florida resident's entire equity in a personal residence may be protected from the claims of a creditor, if the physician lives inside of a city, the debtor can only protect one-half of an acre of land from the claims of a creditor. If the physician resides outside of a municipality, the acreage that may be protected increases to up to 160 acres of contiguous land. Understanding how exemptions work is critical in wealth-protection planning.

Forms of Ownership. Real estate and personal property can be held in various forms of ownership that either put an asset beyond the reach of a creditor or make the asset less desirable for a creditor to seize and realize full value. For instance, some states permit married couples to own property in *tenancy by the entirety*. In most states where property can be owned in this manner, a creditor would need a judgment against *both* spouses to seize the asset held in tenancy by the entireties to satisfy its judgment. Thus, if a physician and his or her spouse own a piece of real estate as tenants by the entirety and the physician has a malpractice judgment against him or her, the creditor cannot seize the property to satisfy the malpractice creditor's judgment. Of course, if the physician's spouse dies unexpectedly, the entire value of the property will vest solely in the physician as the surviving tenant. In this case the physician's creditor could seize the property to satisfy its claim. Divorce could produce a similar result. If the physician's spouse survives the physician, the physician's creditor would have no right to seize the property to satisfy its claim.

Although other forms of co-ownership of property with others, in whatever form, will not produce the same creditor protection result as property held in tenancy by the entireties, this does not mean that such property will be an attractive asset to a creditor. For instance, if Dr. X has a malpractice judgment against him, his one-half tenancy in common interest with Mr. Y might not be an attractive asset to seize because the creditor would share control of the property with Mr. Y.

What is clear is that the way an affluent physician owns assets is critical. Astute asset-protection planning ensures that the assets are owned in the most unattractive manner from a creditor's viewpoint.

Use of Business Entities to Hold Property. Conducting business through a limited liability entity structure could also help avoid liability. Such entities may include limited liability partnerships, limited liability companies and corporations. If structured and administered properly, each of the foregoing entities can preclude personal liability.

For example, Dr. X is in practice with Dr. Y and Dr. Z (the "XYZ Medical Corporation"). If Dr. Y commits malpractice in a matter that does not involve Dr. X, a creditor should not be able to reach Dr. X's personal assets if Dr. Y and the corporation do not have sufficient assets to satisfy the creditor's judgment. Of course, this structure will not protect the value of the assets of the practice, including office equipment and receivables.

Restructuring the Medical Practice. An often-overlooked area of creditor protection for physicians involves restructuring their medical practices. For example, Dr. A and Dr. B practice in A & B, P.A., a professional medical corporation. Although each physician owns 50 percent of the shares of the corporation, each physician is compensated based on the physician's production within the firm. In other words, the corporation never makes a profit distribution *pro rata* to its shareholders. Instead each physician receives a bi-weekly salary distribution based solely on the physician's production. If Dr. A works 500 more hours per year than Dr. B, Dr. A will receive substantially greater compensation in the form of income distributions. Dr. A and Dr. B share all expenses related to their medical corporation equally. Dr. A will cover for Dr. B and *vice versa* when one is on vacation or has a day off. Other than providing coverage, Dr. A and Dr. B do not share patients and rarely consult with each other on patient files.

Suppose Dr. B is sued for an alleged act of malpractice. In this case, the portion of Dr. A's receivables that generates Dr. A's high income becomes subject to the potential creditor's claim. The other assets of the practice also become subject to such claim. Given the nature of Dr. A and Dr. B's relationship, Dr. A (and Dr. B) could avoid this potential liability pitfall by splitting up the practice into two separate medical corporations. Dr. A and Dr. B could continue to practice under the same roof with a similar coverage relationship, and if the corporate restructuring is carefully designed, Dr. A and Dr. B can protect their receivables and other assets used in the practice from the claims of each other's potential creditors.

Asset-Protection Trusts. In general terms, a classic asset-protection trust is a "self-settled trust," that is, a trust where the individual (a "settlor") who creates and funds the trust remains a discretionary beneficiary of the trust. Under the laws of most states such a trust would not be an effective asset-protection device because any creditor could pierce the trust and reach its assets to the maximum extent that a trustee could distribute assets to the settlor. Notwithstanding the foregoing rule, a handful of states (that is, Alaska, Delaware, Missouri, Nevada, Rhode Island, South Dakota and Utah) and most English common-law jurisdictions outside of the United States have a different rule that permits a settlor to create an asset-protection trust, remain a beneficiary, and if the trust is created under appropriate circumstances, the laws of such jurisdiction will shield the assets in such a trust from a settlor's creditors.

Some of the most common offshore jurisdictions to establish asset-protection trusts include the Bahamas, the Cook Islands, Nevis and Belize although there are literally over sixty jurisdictions outside the United States that can be used to establish such a trust. If established in an appropriate manner, an offshore asset-protection trust can be the most effective, efficient and flexible strategy available to protect wealth.

Domestic asset-protection trusts are relatively new in the asset-protection world, and the domestic jurisdictions mentioned above only recently passed legislation permitting an individual to establish such a trust. The oldest domestic asset-protection trust law only dates back to 1997, and at present there have not been any test cases under any of the domestic acts. Numerous questions exist about whether such trusts will withstand scrutiny under various constitutional issues or survive a bankruptcy proceeding. Other theories also exist to attack such trusts. If one seeks a higher level of certainty and an asset-protection trust makes sense, strong consideration should be given to establishing a foreign trust over a domestic trust.

Gifting Assets. Gifting cash or other assets to a spouse, children and grandchildren is a simple, yet effective asset-protection technique. This technique will be most effective if the affluent physician makes gifts when he or she does not have any creditor issues (that is, "when the coast is clear"). Gifts made when the coast is clear are unlikely to raise an issue under applicable fraudulent-transfer laws.

The amount of gifts that an affluent physician decides to make are generally constrained by two factors: gift tax considerations (see Chapter 7, "Advanced Estate Planning") and his or her personal comfort level. A married physician could potentially make up to $2,000,000 in gifts under the lifetime gift-tax exemption and up to $22,000 annually in gifts to third parties without incurring any gift tax. In addition to the foregoing, if properly structured, any affluent physician may make unlimited gifts to or for the benefit of his or her spouse or to or for the benefit of one or more designated charities. The gift-tax laws provide a marital deduction and a charitable deduction for the entire value of any cash or other assets given to a spouse or charity, provided the gift is made in a qualified manner such an outright gift to a spouse or charity or a gift to a marital trust.

Comfort level is also important. No individual wants to transfer so much wealth that he or she jeopardizes his or her own financial security.

For the ultrawealthy physician there are several gifting techniques that can be used for asset protection and enable him or her to transfer wealth without incurring gift tax, even when he or she has exhausted his or her gift-tax exemption and utilized all of his or her annual exclusion benefits. These leveraged gifting techniques include a variety of strategies that, if implemented properly, can protect effectively protect wealth. Such strategies include charitable lead annuity trusts, grantor-retained annuity trusts, private annuity transactions and installment sales. Such strategies also tend to make sense from an estate planning standpoint, that is, a valid non-asset-protection planning reason to utilize such strategies (see Chapter 7, "Advanced Estate Planning").

We often need to go to great pains in helping affluent physicians decide the form in which to make gifts. For instance, a gift to a child who is also a physician could be made to a wholly discretionary trust for the child and his or her children. If the trust is designed properly it should be protected from the claims of any of the child's creditors, whether such creditors exist when the gift is made or arise later. A gift to a spouse could be made to a marital trust. The gift to the trust may protect the property from a future creditor of the physician, and if the physician survives his or her spouse, the trust could actually be designed to return its assets to the physician or be held in further trust for his or her financial benefit and security.

Structuring Gifts and Inheritance to a Physician. We regularly see affluent physicians who expect to receive an inheritance from one or both of his or her parents or another relative. Even small sums of money can be protected if left in the proper format for a physician. An individual in a high-risk profession such as a medicine should consider asking parents and other relatives who may make significant gifts or leave more than a nominal inheritance to make such a gift or leave such an inheritance in a trust for his or her benefit rather than giving such gift or leaving such inheritance to him or her outright, that is, in his or her own name. The trust can be designed as a discretionary trust and include a spendthrift provision and other provisions that would best protect the assets held in the trust.

Conclusion

According to the general public, all physicians or nearly all physicians are wealthy. This, coupled with an "it's not my fault mentality," makes physicians prime targets for unjust lawsuits. Add to these gold diggers, business creditors, jilted lovers and the like and we find affluent physicians squarely in the crosshairs.

The solution for combating unjust lawsuits is asset-protection planning. It's a wise move for affluent physicians to structure their wealth in a way to ward off potential creditors, disillusioned ex-spouses and the like. Regrettably, relatively few affluent physicians have up-to-date asset-protection plans. If they find this out by experience, they have found out too late the magnitude of this mistake.

FINANCIAL WEALTH-PRESERVATION STRATEGIES

With Frank W. Seneco

Cautionary Tale #1 | Failing to Update a Buy/Sell Agreement

Three young physicians started their medical practice 20 years ago. Each contributed an equal amount to the partnership to get started with office help, medical equipment and so forth. The physicians also had a buy/sell agreement written in the event that one of them died prematurely. They used term life insurance to fund the death benefit because of its low cost, with $250,000 of coverage each for the death buyout provision of the buy/sell agreement.

Over the years the practice grew substantially. They expanded their office staff and now have four medical offices. Suggestions were made to update the buy/sell agreement, but because of the doctors' busy schedules they never followed up on the suggestion.

One of the physicians passed away in an automobile accident. Per the buy/sell agreement, the two surviving physicians have an obligation to buy out their deceased partner's interest in the medical practice from his heirs.

The practice is now worth $15 million at fair market value. The outdated buy/sell states that the value for buyout purposes on death is the amount of the life insurance. Thus, the surviving spouse had to sell her $5 million interest in the practice for $250,000. This looks like a clear case for a lawsuit by the spouse against the practice. Although the court of equity would rule in her favor, there have been cases just like this brought to trial and the terms of the written agreement prevailed.

Cautionary Tale #2 | Failing to Review the Funding of a Buy/Sell Agreement

Another medical practice started by three physicians also had a buy/sell agreement. However, this agreement stated that the buyout amount was the fair market value of the medical practice at the time of death, which would be determined by an outside valuation company. In this case, one third of the practice is worth $5 million but there was only $300,000 of life insurance.

The surviving partners now must pay off the required amount to the deceased partner's heirs through current cash flow. This puts a tremendous burden on their medical practice. Each surviving partner had to support not only the ongoing medical practice but had to provide additional funds to pay off the buy/sell agreement requirements. Here is a situation where each survivor had to put in a greater effort for a decreased reward.

Cautionary Tale #3 | Failure to Prepare For Becoming Disabled

Dr. Jones has one partner in his medical practice. He was earning approximately $1 million per year. He and his partner had the practice valued at $10 million, and they had updated their buy/sell arrangement to reflect the current fair market value of the business. They put in place adequate life insurance to cover the buyout in the event of a partner's death. However, they decided not to fund buyout insurance in the event either of them became permanently disabled. They felt the premiums for the disability insurance were too high.

A year later Dr. Jones was diving off his lake-house pier with his children. He unfortunately slipped on his last dive and went headfirst into shallow water. He suffered severe neck and spinal injuries and later learned he was quadriplegic, making it impossible for him to work. His partner was obligated to buy him out of the practice, but there was no funding in place to do it. This put a tremendous strain on Dr. Jones, as he had to deal with how and when he would get his fair value of the business he helped build, as well as the strain on his partner to fund his obligation to buy out his partner and continue the business. Here is another case of the survivor working harder and getting less for the effort.

———————————

In the world of advanced planning, when we talk about financial strategies we are dealing with strategies that are predicated on financial products. Although some estate and asset-protection planning strategies incorporate financial products such as life insurance and derivatives, they are often considered secondary to the legal maneuvering. In contrast, with financial strategies, the financial products take a more prominent position. Admittedly, in practice, this distinction can become a little fuzzy.

In this chapter, we will be considering:

- How affluent physicians can prepare for the forced transition of equity positions in their practices. These would be defined as estate planning strategies in our advanced planning taxonomy.
- How affluent physicians can free operating capital from their accounts receivable and protect these monies against future litigants. This is usually defined as an asset-protection strategy.

In the following chapter, we will discuss another financial strategy to protect assets—using a captive insurance company, which can also result in decrease premiums and even generate additional future income. As with all the strategies we discussed so far, we are only going to highlight them, and it's important to remember that their viability is dependent on each affluent physician's particular situation.

Forced Equity Transitions

When an affluent physician has an equity stake in a medical practice and he or she dies or is disabled, the adverse financial repercussion for the rest of the equity holders in the medical practice can be severe. Generally, there is a need to buy out the disabled physician or to buy out the heirs of the deceased physician. The quandary is when preparations have not been made for these possible scenarios or the preparations are inadequate. As we saw in the cautionary tales at the beginning of the chapter, failing to prepare adequately for forced financial transitions can potentially eradicate a medical practice and can even result in costly lawsuits.

Forced equity transitions occur when a physician with an equity stake in the medical practice dies or becomes seriously disabled and he or she has equity partners. In looking at our sample of affluent physicians we found that 79.5 percent of them are in this situation (Exhibit 9.1). They are equity partners with other physicians in a medical practice. This is more indicative of the less wealthy physicians (81.5 percent compared to 69.1 percent).

Exhibit 9.1 | Have an Equity Stake in a Medical Practice With Others

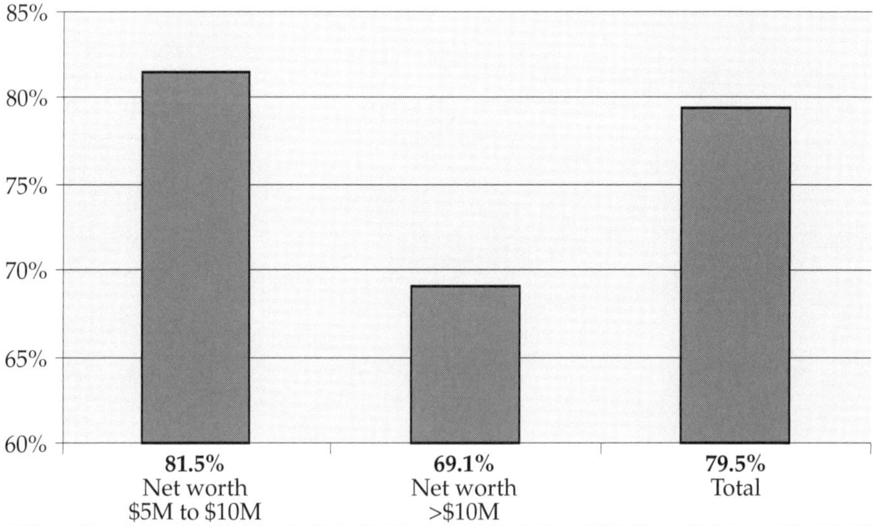

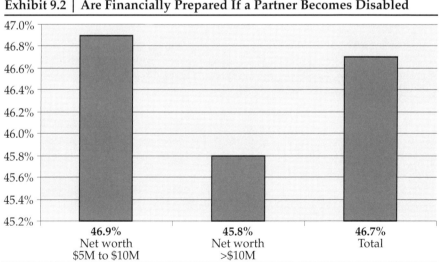

| 81.5% | 69.1% | 79.5% |
| Net worth $5M to $10M | Net worth >$10M | Total |

N = 941 Affluent Physicians

Looking at those affluent physicians sharing equity with other physicians in a medical practice, we found that 46.7 percent are financially prepared to deal with a physician partner becoming disabled (Exhibit 9.2). The difference between the two wealth segments was negligible.

Exhibit 9.2 | Are Financially Prepared If a Partner Becomes Disabled

| 46.9% | 45.8% | 46.7% |
| Net worth $5M to $10M | Net worth >$10M | Total |

N = 670 Affluent Physicians

We also found that relatively speaking more affluent physicians (55.1 percent) are financially prepared if a physician equity partner dies (Exhibit 9.3). Again, the difference between the two wealth segments was negligible.

Exhibit 9.3 | Are Financially Prepared If a Partner Dies

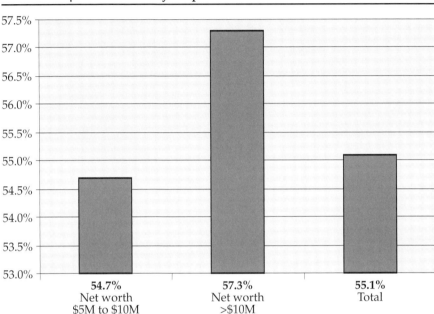

54.7%	57.3%	55.1%
Net worth	Net worth	Total
$5M to $10M	>$10M	

N = 670 Affluent Physicians

Turning to factor analysis to identify the <u>principal motivations</u> for not being financially prepared in these situations, we found that the motivations for not being prepared for the injury or death of a physician equity partner parallel each other (Exhibit 9.4). For a little more than half the affluent physicians (54.4 percent not prepared for injury; 55.5 percent not prepared for death) the cost of being financially prepared was deemed too high.

Nearly a quarter of the physicians (22.1 percent not prepared for injury; 23.6 percent not prepared for death) believe if these tragedies do occur they can work it out. Although this is a very noble sentiment, in our experience it just never seems to happen—at least without lawyers present.

About one in ten physicians (11.8 percent not prepared for injury; 11.3 percent not prepared for death) are too busy to deal with the matter at the present time. And for similar percentages of affluent physicians (11.7 percent not prepared for injury; 9.6 percent not prepared for death) the issue is not on their radar screens.

Exhibit 9.4 | Reason Affluent Physicians Are Not Financially Prepared

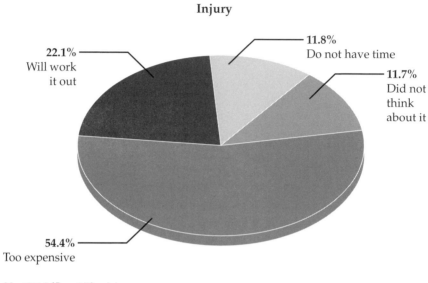

Injury

22.1%
Will work
it out

11.8%
Do not have time

11.7%
Did not
think
about it

54.4%
Too expensive

N = 357 Affluent Physicians

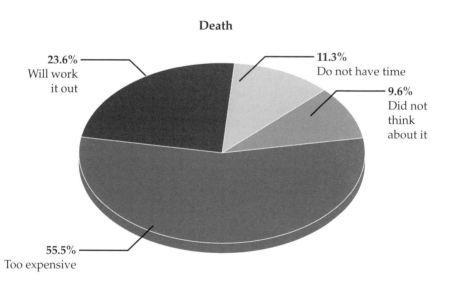

Death

23.6%
Will work
it out

11.3%
Do not have time

9.6%
Did not
think
about it

55.5%
Too expensive

N = 301 Affluent Physicians

Often the easiest way to manage these potential disasters is with disability and life insurance. As we have seen, cost is the biggest issue. Moreover, in our experience, when the expense of purchasing disability and life insurance to deal with these matters is effectively managed, we find that those affluent physicians who initially felt that they would just work it out choose to formalize the arrangement.

The key is how to most efficaciously purchase the proper amount of each kind of insurance. To avoid a forced financial transition, it is advantageous to set up a buy/sell agreement and cover two possibilities—disability and death.

Disability. Considering that many physicians are financially fragile (see Chapter 2, "Sources of Financial Dissatisfaction Among Affluent Physicians"), having disability insurance is usually a very wise move. In general, disability insurance tends to be "tricky." From defining what constitutes a disability to programming disability benefits, affluent physicians getting what they want and need can be problematic. What we have found is that the issue is having enough affordable disability insurance.

Aside from a physician having disability insurance to provide income for a period of time while injured, there are a variety of types of disability policies. One type that should usually be considered by solo practitioners or physicians in a small group is business-overhead disability. Business-overhead coverage will pay a monthly benefit to cover business expenses while the physician is disabled. We have found that many physicians look to this type of coverage when they can no longer obtain personal disability coverage.

For those affluent physicians who have equity in a larger medical group, we recommend examining disability insurance in a buy/sell agreement. With such a strategy in place, it's possible for a disabled physician who is entitled to a share of the group's revenue to be cost-effectively bought out. Thus, there is not a disabling financial drain on the rest of the equity partners in the medical group.

Based on the buy/sell arrangement, there are, in general, three possible ways to for the disabled physicians to collect:

- A lump-sum payment usually available after a waiting period often lasting two years
- A series of annuity payments over a specified period of time, which is often two to five years after a waiting period of one to two years
- A combination of the above two

The cost of disability insurance is a function of the amount of the coverage, the physician's specialty, the length of the waiting period and the length of the payout period. The more coverage, the more it costs. The level of risks associated with a physician's specialty is also a big factor in determining the cost of the disability insurance. For instance, anesthesiologists are more likely to become disabled than general practitioners, thereby making disability insurance for them more expensive.

As noted, the longer the waiting period and the longer the payout period, the lower the premiums will be. The waiting period is defined as the period of time from the date of the accident or illness causing the disability to the time the benefit payments start.

Disability buy/sell agreements are fairly straightforward. The critical element is to keep them up-to-date and properly funded. For affluent physicians, as well as many we would not define as affluent, the complication is being able to obtain sufficient disability coverage at manageable costs. This situation can, depending on circumstances, be dealt with by employing a captive insurance company (see Chapter 10, "Leveraging Captive Insurance Companies").

Death. Few physicians want the heirs of a deceased partner to have equity in their medical practice. Nevertheless, we find that this does indeed occasionally come to pass. When advanced preparations for such a possibility are not taken, the physicians are in the difficult position of having to buy out the heirs. We have seen negotiations to buy out heirs become quite messy as emotions tend to override business sense.

As with an injured physician, a buy/sell agreement on an equity partner's death is commonly the most viable strategy. Here, the heirs exchange their equity in the medical practice for a lump-sum payment.

Once it is determined that life insurance is needed, the question of how to pay for it arises. Several different methods can be used to fund the life insurance part of the buy/sell agreement.

The individual physician can pay for his or her own policy out of his or her after-tax income. The reasoning for this approach is that the families of each doctor will benefit from the life insurance policy, so it is in each physician's best interest to fund it.

The alternative is for the medical practice to pay the premiums on the life insurance. One way to do this is to have the medical practice pay out a bonus to the physician in the amount of the premium. The physician's cost is the income tax on the bonus. If the practice is a tax passthrough entity such as a partnership or limited liability company, then there may be a passthrough tax that the premium payment represents. Each situation should be evaluated with all the tax consequences taken into consideration before using a bonus plan.

Additional funding options are available, however, they tend to become more complicated from here on out. Life insurance, for instance, can be purchased through a Section 412(i) qualified retirement plan with pretax dollars. Because we are dealing with a qualified retirement plan, rules are in control and as a result, there are limitations on the amount of the death benefit. A further requirement is that all employees must be allowed to participate in some form in the plan. However, with a Section 412(i) qualified retirement plan it is also possible to enhance significantly the retirement benefits for participating physicians compared to many other types of qualified retirement plans. And some if not all of the premiums on the life insurance policy can be purchased using tax-deductible dollars.

There are other strategies that we can use to mitigate the out-of-pocket costs of paying the premiums for the life insurance used to fund buy/sell agreements. One entails using equity split-dollar plans to loan money to the policy owner, who then pays the premiums with the loans, which are secured by the life insurance policy. Another entails using outside sources to fund the life insurance policy so that the out-of-pocket costs are marginalized. In the appropriate situations, the medical practice's accounts receivable can be utilized as a way to pay for the premiums on the life insurance policy.

Ongoing monitoring. What we repeatedly see is that most buy/sell agreements funded with either disability or life insurance do not cover the true costs of the equity owned by the injured or deceased physician partner. What is happening is that the physicians set up buy/sell agreements and fund them with the proper amount of insurance. However, over time, the value of the medical practice or the revenues generated by the medical practice has substantially increased, making the amounts of insurance purchased inadequate.

Although buy/sell agreements are legal agreements, they do not halt a lawsuit by the injured physician or the heirs of the deceased physician. Therefore, we review with our affluent-physician clients the need, structuring and amount of coverage of their buy/sell agreements on a regular basis. What we tend to find is that as the medical practices grow, we are able to find greater cost-effective ways to obtain more coverage.

It's important to note that there are other advanced planning strategies that can be employed to deal with forced equity transitions. For instance, the use of structured products can prove very effective instead of buy/sell agreements. However, there are limited times when structured products will be more efficacious than the less costly buy/sell agreement. Therefore, like all aspects of advanced planning, the particulars of the affluent-physician client's situation drive the possibilities.

Protecting Accounts Receivable

Most physicians have considerable monies they have yet to be paid. According to our research, 70.8 percent of affluent physicians say they have meaningful accounts receivable (Exhibit 9.5). This is more the case with the less wealthy physicians (76.3 percent compared to 69.7 percent).

Exhibit 9.5 | Affluent Physicians With Meaningful Accounts Receivable

78%
76%
74%
72%
70%
68%
66%
69.7%
Net worth
$5M to $10M
76.3%
Net worth
>$10M
70.8%
Total

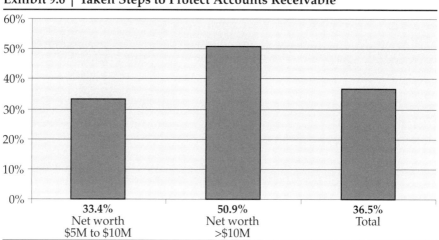

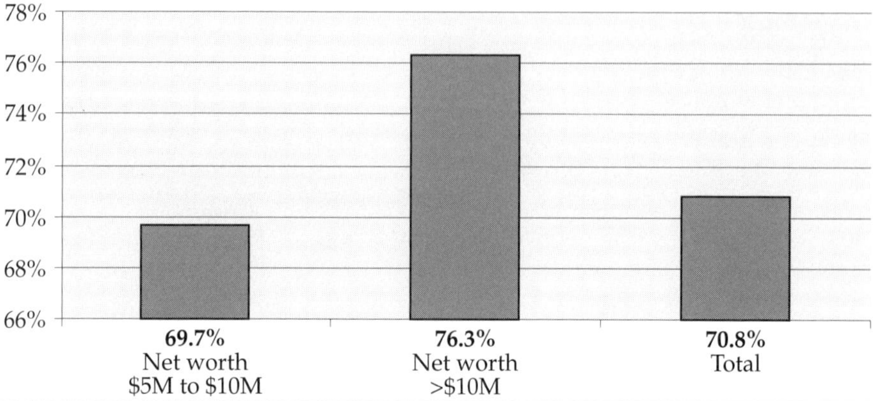

N = 941 Affluent Physicians

These funds are potentially the most easily accessible monies to a litigant. With respect to a well-running practice, a creditor has to often just wait for the accounts receivable to come in to collect on a judgment. The complication for the practice is paying expenses such as salaries when these funds are not available.

Although 70.8 percent of the affluent-physician practices have meaningful accounts receivable, only 36.5 percent of them have taken steps to protect these monies (Exhibit 9.6). It's the wealthier physicians who have taken the initiative (50.9 percent compared to 33.4 percent).

Exhibit 9.6 | Taken Steps to Protect Accounts Receivable

60%
50%
40%
30%
20%
10%
0%
33.4%
Net worth
$5M to $10M
50.9%
Net worth
>$10M
36.5%
Total

N = 587 Affluent Physicians

One of the most effective ways of protecting accounts receivable is by encumbering them. This approach, known as equity stripping, is also used to protect real estate from creditors.

The idea is to take out a loan using the accounts receivable as the security. Depending on the situation, it's possible to obtain a loan for 100 percent of the monies outstanding. Furthermore, with this strategy, the interest the physician practice is charged is quite favorable.

The loan proceeds are not taxable. Meanwhile, the interest payments on the loan are tax-deductible. This effectively lowers the cost of borrowing the money. From an asset-protection view, at this point, we have actually made the situation worse. The cash is more vulnerable than the accounts receivable.

The medical practice can take either of the following generic actions:
• The loan proceeds can be distributed to the equity partners in the practice. The distributions are therefore taxable to the partners.
• The loan proceeds can be used to fund retirement benefits. These proceeds can fund either qualified or nonqualified plans.

It often proves a wise move to incorporate life insurance into the retirement plan being funded by the loan proceeds. This is more the case if the physicians are opting for a nonqualified benefit plan. The life insurance policy itself can also provide creditor protection based on the laws of the state in which the practice operates.

If the life insurance policy is performing well, it's very likely that the physicians can actually make money by using this strategy. If this is the case, after a period of time tax-free loans from the internal build-up in the life insurance policy are used to pay off the original accounts receivable loan. Instead of paying off the original loan or after doing so, the monies in the life insurance policies can be used for additional income for the partners at their discretion.

What can readily happen is that, using this advanced planning strategy, a physician practice can protect its accounts receivable as well as enhance the wealth of its partners.

Conclusion

We find it scary the number of medical groups we see that are financially ravaged because one of the partner physicians has become disabled or died. This potential disaster is easily rectified by a little planning and preparation.

Along similar lines, many medical groups fail to protect their assets effectively, with accounts receivable being an asset that plays a big role in most medical practices. There are a number of ways to protect accounts receivable so as to benefit the physicians in a medical practice.

LEVERAGING CAPTIVE INSURANCE COMPANIES

With Stuart H. Anolik

Increasingly the wealthy are employing captive insurance companies to preserve their fortunes. From mitigating business risks tax-efficiently to mitigating personal risks tax-efficiently, captive insurance companies—when properly implemented and managed—can be wonderful tools for the affluent and the firms they run and/or own.

For over 50 years, captive insurance companies have been available as an alternative to traditional insurance companies. Conservatively, there are now over 5,000 organizations that have chosen to use a captive insurance company as part of their risk-financing strategies. Nearly half of all major hospital groups have at least one captive, with the number of physician-owned captives on a steady rise.

A number of states such as Pennsylvania, Florida, Mississippi, Nevada, Texas, New Jersey, West Virginia, New York, Ohio and Illinois are in a medical malpractice liability crisis according to the American Medical Association. Neurology, obstetrics, cardiology and orthopedics are examples of the specialties that have been hit hard. Numerous legislative proposals have been considered, and President Bush is promoting tort reform. Physicians have threatened to leave the practice due to prohibitive insurance rates. The practice of "defensive medicine" is driving up health-care costs. Creative and flexible malpractice insurance products are needed to fill the void. For some medical practices and hospitals, captive insurance companies are the answer.

Just what is a captive insurance company?

A captive insurance company is a closely held insurance company whose insurance business is primarily supplied by a select clientele who are taking the risk.

Some captive insurance companies are owned and operated by the firm being insured. Sometimes a number of firms group together to employ the captive insurance model. Typically, these firms are in the same line of business such as such as OBGYN physicians, construction companies or law firms, to name a few.

Another variation is where a captive insurance company rents its capital, surplus and legal capacity to organizations. The sponsor controls the captive insurance company and generally designs a program where the insured party obtains benefits that are equivalent to those provided by the standard forms of a captive insurance company without participating in the ownership or management—or cost—of managing the captive insurance company or its capital-adequacy requirements. The sponsor usually provides administrative services, reinsurance and/or an admitted fronting company, if necessary.

A relatively recent innovation is the *cell captive*. It is a single legal entity composed of individual protected cells. The assets of one cell are not subject to claims of/against other cells. Therefore, a medical group can potentially rent a cell, thereby segregating out its own risk.

Captive insurance companies can be formed and licensed within the United States or in an offshore jurisdiction. A captive can be used to provide predictability in insurance coverage and premiums, insure risks that would otherwise need to be self-insured, or to provide supplemental insurance. Additionally, deductibles, exclusions and coverage that are difficult to obtain at a reasonable price are all examples of the types of risks that can be shifted to a captive insurance company.

Benefits of a Captive Insurance Company

There are numerous benefits to using a captive insurance company. They include:

- Cost savings
- Access to the reinsurance market
- Coverage availability
- Sharing in investment income
- Cash-flow management
- Control
- Tax advantages

Let's now take a closer look at these benefits.

Cost savings. A captive insurance company is almost always cheaper to operate than a conventional insurer. Thus, a captive insurance company can either provide lower premiums or build reserves for future premium reductions or the eventual return of capital to its users. Furthermore, when renting a captive insurance company that includes the cell-captive model, a medical practice or hospital rents the capital of the sponsor and uses the sponsor's infrastructure for items such as an annual audit and claims handling procedures, thereby reducing overall expenses.

Access to the reinsurance market. A captive insurance company has access to the reinsurance market. Because captive insurance companies are not in the public commercial market looking for individual customers, reinsurance companies work on lower expense ratios than direct insurers. Thus, reinsurance may be obtained at a lower cost than conventional direct insurance. Commissions may also be earned on the reinsurance ceded, which may also reduce the overall cost of insurance.

Coverage availability. Cyclical changes in the insurance markets, poor underwriting results, and a reluctance to insure certain risks may cause some lines of insurance to be unavailable, available at a prohibitive cost, or available on extremely restrictive terms. A captive insurance company may be the only realistic way to insure such risks. For example, it may be difficult to obtain practice-continuation coverage on the key physicians in a practice. However, when structured through the captive insurance company, it becomes possible to insure this risk.

Sharing in investment income. Premiums and reserves may be invested for the benefit of the captive insurance company. In conventional insurance the investment income is profit for the insurer. With a captive insurance company, the physicians can share in the investment income. Furthermore, depending on the structuring, many insurance companies need not pay tax on their investment income, thereby effectively increasing the returns it earns on its capital.

Cash-flow management. The payment of premiums can be tailored to the requirement of the medical group or hospital. This can result in superior cash-flow management.

Control. Greater control may be exercised on risk management issues such as loss control, loss reporting procedures and safety programs, which may result in a reduction in frequency and severity of claims. In addition, the captive insurance company may adopt a more focused approach to claims settlements than a third-party insurer. The captive insurance company and the physicians, rather than the big, impersonal insurance company, determines what cases to litigate, what cases to settle and what strategy to take in any dispute.

Tax advantages. The proper structure of a captive insurance company and the conduct of its business may produce key tax benefits. Premiums paid to the captive by the medical practice may be tax-deductible, the receipt of the premiums by the captive insurance company may be tax-advantaged due to the deductibility of a captive insurance company's discounted reserves, and the reserves build up free of income taxes. Tax planning in relation to a captive insurance facility is complex but can be very rewarding.

Disadvantages of Captive Insurance Companies

There are two principle disadvantages to captive insurance companies. One disadvantage is the cost and time involved in setting them up and operating them. Formation costs and operating costs can be prohibitive for a stand-alone wholly owned captive insurance company. It typically takes six to nine months to form a captive insurance company. Formation includes feasibility studies, a business plan and licensing in the domicile of choice. The cost of formation is approximately $60,000 to $85,000 or more—sometimes much more. In addition to the costs of formation, capital, which is usually around $250,000 or more, is also required. Annual operating costs are $50,000 and up and this does not include ancillary legal and audit fees.

Renting a captive insurance company can substantially reduce the time and cost of obtaining the benefits of a captive insurance company. The costs of renting are usually a percentage of the premium to be charged (generally 7 to 10 percent) and the time involved could be as a little as two weeks. Annual operating costs are also typically a percentage of the premiums and reserves built up (anywhere between 2 and 5 percent).

Another disadvantage of captive insurance companies is their complexity. A captive is a complex corporate structure to form and maintain and involves significant tax and corporate governance issues. Maintenance of a captive facility requires extensive expertise. This is where many users of captive insurance companies have run aground. If the captive is not set up just right and managed just right, there are going to be problems—potentially severe, business-ravaging problems.

Physician Involvement

The captive model requires physicians to take control over the risk management of the practice. After all, physicians will be dealing with their own money, not an insurance company's reserves. Thus, the captive model is not a "write a check and close your eyes" approach to medicine. Because the money in the captive insurance company, after claims and expenses, belongs to the medical groups or hospitals, the captive approach leads to more involvement in risk management by physicians.

Experience shows us that good loss practices become better loss practices, as the physicians typically find more incentive to obtain extra education, take proper precautions, and not take unnecessary risks. Typically, risk management policies are reviewed, modified and adhered to. When this occurs the physicians are able to share in the tax-free growth of the captive's reserves, which enhances their wealth.

For example, a typical practice involved with a captive insurance company will find itself with a program designed to reduce risk. This will involve regular, ongoing risk management education that focuses on such things as documentation, diagnosis and damage control. It also focuses on patient satisfaction. The education program also involves the introduction of new techniques for ensuring that all steps are taken on a regular basis to reduce risk.

The Impact of Taxes

We already touched upon the tax benefits of a captive insurance company. However, the recent changes in legislation and in the position of the IRS have made these tax-advantaged captive insurance companies particularly attractive to medical practices today.

The key issue with captive insurance companies is to ensure that the medical practice can deduct malpractice insurance premiums paid to the captive insurance company. This issue was litigated for numerous years, but the IRS finally issued two Revenue Rulings that provide safe harbors relative to the formation of the captive insurance company and deductibility of premiums paid to the captive insurance company. If the captive insurance company is formed and operated within these safe harbors, then premiums paid to the captive insurance company are deductible.

Premiums received (and investment income thereon) by the captive insurance company in many cases are not subject to tax. In addition, upon a subsequent liquidation of the captive insurance company or the physician's exit from the medical practice, the physician can, under the proper circumstances, obtain monies from the captive insurance company at tax-advantaged rates. Finally, the captive insurance company acts as an asset-protection entity because all the assets therein are protected from claims by third-party creditors.

Choice of Domicile—Domestic or Offshore

Numerous states and offshore jurisdictions have developed captive insurance legislation and are actively promoting their jurisdictions. A domestic captive insurance company requires adherence to its state's insurance regulatory regime and is subject to state premium taxes. An offshore captive insurance company is subject to the offshore jurisdiction's insurance regulatory regime and is not subject to tax. To level the playing field between domestic and offshore captive insurance companies, premiums paid to an offshore captive are subject to a four percent excise tax (1 percent if the premium is for reinsurance). Ownership of an offshore captive insurance company is subject to complex United States tax rules that seek to subject to United States tax income accumulated in the offshore jurisdiction by United States owners.

An offshore captive insurance company can make an election to be treated as a United States insurance company, a section 953(d) election. The benefit of the election exempts the captive insurance company from the federal excise tax and withholding taxes, allows the captive to hold meetings in the United States and to otherwise conduct business in the United States, and allows the captive insurance company to invest more freely in United States assets.

Deciding on whether to use a domestic or offshore captive insurance company can be a complicated matter. It will depend, very much, on the particular situation.

Case Study #1 | Virginia Emergency Room Physicians

In Virginia, the legislature has provided a hard cap for damages for malpractice. The cap adjusts annually and is currently approximately $1.8 million. The hospitals have responded by requiring the physicians to carry malpractice insurance up to this limit. However, compared to other parts of the country, malpractice premiums are not so bad, as a Virginia emergency room physician can obtain malpractice insurance in the amount of $2 million/$6 million for approximately $25,000.

A group of 41 emergency room physicians are paying an annual premium of approximately $1.95 million. The group routinely pays this insurance, which has been escalating annually. On average, the group has seen annual losses of about $800,000. This leaves the insurance company with $1.15 million for administration and profit.

Due to the large limits and the unlikelihood of claims in excess of $1 million, this group was a good candidate for a slow shift to a captive insurance company. Initially, the group lowered its limits by half to $1 million/$3 million from $2 million/$6 million, thereby saving approximately 15 percent to 20 percent of the premium or about $390,000 per year. Using the $390,000 a year in savings by lowering the limits, the group began funding a captive insurance program.

This excess insurance premium (the $390,000) will continue to build up with a very limited likelihood of being used for claims. Each annual payment of $390,000 is tax-deductible, and the monies will grow tax-free within the captive insurance company. After several years, the emergency room physician medical group will build up a few million dollars in reserves. There are a number of possible uses of these reserves, including:

- The ability to rely solely on the captive insurance company for malpractice insurance
- The ability to use the reserves to legally contest cases the medical malpractice insurance company will not

- The opportunity to let the reserves grow tax-free so, with a good claims history, these funds would be available to the medical group and/or the individual physicians in the future, rather than padding the bottom line of a commercial insurance company

In the case of a good claims history, the medical group and/or the individual physicians are able to, under the proper circumstances, take the monies out of the captive insurance company. These funds are taxed as ordinary income, but they were growing tax-free and were a legitimate business expense when they were put into the captive insurance company. There are circumstances where the physicians can recover the reserves and pay less then their personal income tax rates.

When we compare the two approaches—using traditional malpractice insurance and leveraging a captive insurance company—we find that over five years, without any changes in medical malpractice premiums, the emergency room physician medical group will pay out $9.75 million. In comparison, by employing the captive insurance company as we have described, the medical group will still pay $1.56 million to the traditional malpractice insurance company for a five-year total of $7.8 million. At the same time, the annual payments of $390,000 placed in the captive insurance company—after all fees and an investment growth rate of 5 percent—results in $1.9 million in the captive (Exhibit 10.1).

Exhibit 10.1 | Five-Year Comparison

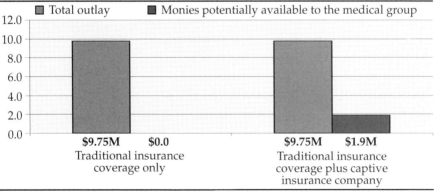

In sum, by limiting the primary insurance and placing the excess into a captive insurance company, the medical practice has been able to accumulate almost $2 million in reserves. At this point, the medical practice has the opportunity to either continue its current course or switch to a full captive solution. Additionally, the medical practice could completely switch to the captive insurance company and use reinsurance to insure against a large loss, such as one over $1 million. By maintaining lower limits on the medical practice's primary commercial coverage, the primary commercial carrier will be responsible for any and all defense costs and losses up to $1 million per occurrence. This allows the captive insurance company's premiums and reserves to be preserved, unless and until there is a loss in excess of the $1 million per-occurrence limit.

Let's say at this point—after the five years where the captive has been in use—the emergency room physician group disbands. Let's also assume there have not been any claims in excess of $1 million and that each physician receives an equal share of the monies in the captive insurance company. This will then result in additional income for each physician of slightly more than $46,000.

Case Study #2 | Florida Neurosurgeons

Unlike Virginia, malpractice rates in Florida have skyrocketed. A Florida neurosurgeon will pay a premium of approximately $75,000 for $200,000/$600,000 in malpractice insurance. Given the rather small amount of insurance compared to the premium, a Florida neurosurgeon medical practice is a good fit to move directly into a captive environment. It can immediately move its entire premium into the captive insurance company, build up reserves over the years, and have plenty of reserves available for any claims under the $200,000/$600,000 limits.

In a medical group of six neurosurgeons, each physician was paying $75,000 per year for malpractice insurance for an annual total of $450,000 per year. After five years they will have paid $2.25 million for medical malpractice insurance.

By switching to a captive insurance company, assuming loss and defense fees of $100,000 in each of years three, four and five; subtracting all fees; and assuming an investment growth rate of 5 percent, at the end of the five years the neurosurgeons will have accumulated $1.1 million in the captive insurance company (Exhibit 10.2).

Exhibit 10.2 | Five-Year Comparison

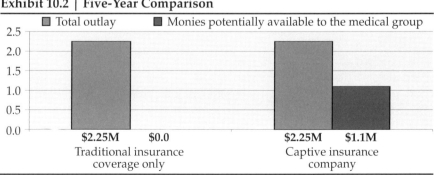

$2.25M $0.0	$2.25M $1.1M
Traditional insurance coverage only	Captive insurance company

Thus, this medical practice will still retain the necessary insurance through the captive insurance company, and at the end of five years will have built up $1.1 million in reserves. These are funds that the physicians will be able to use to either fund premiums in later years, increase coverage, or make a return of premium payments to themselves (depending upon loss history). Looking at the last option, if the neurosurgeons decided to disband their group and return the monies in the captive insurance company to themselves, each physician will receive more than $180,000.

Additional Uses of Captive Insurance Companies for Medical Groups

Captive insurance companies are proving very worthwhile for many medical groups, and this trend is likely to intensify in the current health care and litigation-happy environment we are living in. Dealing with medical malpractice costs notwithstanding, captive insurance companies can be used by affluent physicians and medical groups in other ways.

We are increasingly seeing captive insurance companies being used to deal with the problem of a physician partner in a thriving medical practice becoming disabled. We talked about the need for disability insurance to buy out an incapacitated physician (see Chapter 9, "Financial Wealth-Preservation Strategies").

The conundrum occurs when the medical group is unable to obtain enough disability insurance at a reasonable cost. This conundrum can potentially be resolved by employing a captive insurance company.

Not only can a disabled physician prove the undoing of a medical practice, other courses of business interruption, such as "acts of God" in the form of natural disasters, can kill a thriving practice. Once again, a captive insurance company might be a viable means of managing these risks. Another use of a captive insurance company is the management of compliance with the Health Insurance Portability and Accountability Act (HIPAA).

What is clear is that a captive insurance company—in expert hands—is a quite versatile and potentially exceedingly powerful tool for affluent physicians and their medical practices. Moreover, because of the flexibility of the captive insurance company, all types of medical groups are able to deal with a variety of situations.

Caveat Emptor Again

As we mentioned above, captive insurance companies are complex. And that complexity can be the undoing of a lifetime of hard work if the wrong advanced planning professionals are put in charge. The case studies we used in this chapter only noted the highlights—the very high highlights.

Each medical group has to be evaluated to determine whether using a captive insurance company is appropriate. In our experience, just as there are a great many medical groups for which the use of captive insurance companies for medical malpractice is a very *good* idea, there are many more medical groups for which the use of captive insurance companies for medical malpractice is a very *bad* idea. Each medical group must be carefully evaluated to determine the viability of employing a captive insurance company.

Because there are unscrupulous advisors promoting captive insurance companies indiscriminately, physicians have to be very careful with whom they work on this matter—as they need to be with respect to any advanced planning strategy.

Conclusion

A captive insurance company can provide physicians with significant benefits including recapture of underwriting profit and investment income, flexibility in program design, broader coverage, access to reinsurance, low program costs and potential cash refunds of premiums in the event of a positive loss history.

In today's litigious environment, the captive insurance company is becoming a very attractive option to supplement and, in some cases, completely replace, traditional malpractice insurance. And we are seeing that even with tort reform—and in some cases because of tort reform—captive insurance companies will become an even more attractive option.

Beyond using captive insurance companies to deal with the matter of malpractice insurance, there are many additional uses for captive insurance companies by affluent physicians and medical groups. The ability of the physician partners to ensure the continuity of their practices when disaster strikes is a prime example of the versatility of the captive insurance company.

The biggest complication in employing captive insurance companies is that they are very complicated and, when improperly established and managed, can be disastrous for physicians. Therefore, as with all advanced planning strategies, the need for highly talented and skilled advisors is a must (see Chapter 6, "Caveat Emptor").

Afterword

WEALTH PRESERVATION AND BEYOND

For an ever greater number of physicians, the ability to become affluent (as we have defined affluent—a net worth of $5 million or more) is likely to become more arduous going forward. With incomes being restrained, astute investing and/or leveraging talents (e.g., inventing and patenting a new heart pump) is likely to be the route to significant wealth.

At the same time, based on analytic modeling, our best estimate is that there are 43,700 affluent physicians today. And, in general, these physicians are very interested in safeguarding their wealth from taxes, litigants and creditors that can be legally avoided. In a nutshell, most affluent physicians are strongly attracted to the idea of wealth preservation. Moreover, less wealthy physicians as well as medical groups can use many of the advanced planning strategies that affluent physicians would employ to preserve their wealth.

It's important to realize that wealth preservation predicated on advanced planning is far from static. As we touched on in Chapter 3, "The Nature of Advanced Planning," the Innovation Process systematically results in new and creative ways for physicians to protect their wealth.

Derivatives, for example, are becoming a feasible way for wealthy individuals to "freeze the value" of selected assets. This, in turn permits the assets to be transferred to heirs or others at a discount to their "true value." The use of derivatives in this context also ensures the assets are protected in case of a judgment against the physician. Although strategies utilizing derivatives in this manner are currently limited to the very wealthy, it's evident that very soon they will be available to physicians who are not especially affluent. Meanwhile, we are involved with affluent clients who are better using the power of derivatives for both estate planning and asset protection. For the exceptionally wealthy in just the right set of circumstances, derivative-based advanced planning strategies are also able to eliminate income taxes for about a decade or two.

We are always evolving advanced planning strategies that incorporate life insurance, because that corner of the world is a "moving target." The rules and regulations as well as the tax environment are in a near-perpetual state of flux. We are now able to—for wealthier clients—enable them to create a family bank in perpetuity by using life insurance purchased at a deep discount. The family bank, when properly structured, is quite versatile. It's a pool of money the wealthy individual's family can access for generations (or forever, if the funds are not depleted) to pay for a variety of "things" such as health care, education costs, property, homes, boats and private jets used by the family. There are many other examples where life insurance can create tremendous financial opportunities, and many more are being and will be developed.

Although we have focused on wealth preservation, it's a mistake not to recognize that advanced planning can provide solutions to other physician financial concerns:

- The ability to create a meaningful pool of monies for physicians in retirement, above and beyond the monies they will have through their qualified retirement plans
- The ability to obtain preferential and premium credit arrangements for medical groups, hospitals and medical firms using special-purpose entities
- The ability to enable physicians and medical groups to make significant charitable gifts that are exponentially greater than they thought was possible
- The ability to attract, retain and motivate nonphysician personnel working in a medical group or hospital by providing long-term incentives and financial "lock-ups" in a cost-effective manner
- The ability to minimize taxes on sweat-equity positions physicians have received in medical firms as well as on income generated from patents
- The ability of physicians to make significant charitable gifts and simultaneously boost up their assets in retirement
- The ability to create tax-free growth of invested monies by placing the assets in a specialized entity designed for that purpose

Advanced planning strategies are not only exceedingly effective in enabling affluent physicians to stay affluent, but they can prove instrumental in enabling affluent physicians to become more monetarily successful. Moving beyond wealth preservation, affluent physicians as well as medical groups often call us to use advanced planning strategies to maximize their wealth.

We are not talking about investing per se when we're involved in wealth maximization. Instead, our emphasis is on strategies and financial products that can create "above-normal" returns for physicians. We have already seen this with respect to captive insurance companies (see Chapter 10, "Leveraging Captive Insurance Companies").

There are a plethora of possibilities to employ advanced planning strategies to maximize wealth. Just look at a few of the possibilities with respect to life insurance: we have private-placement variable life insurance policies, the creation of a family bank that circumvents both estate and gift taxes creating an environment for tax-free growth, as well as annuity/life insurance arbitrage opportunities. In the retirement plan environment we have 412(i) plans, private placement annuities as well as a range of supplemental plans applicable for medical groups and hospitals.

By capitalizing on the laws and regulations, and by leveraging the nuances and fine distinctions in the tax code, physicians are in a wonderful position to not only preserve their wealth but also optimize their wealth. The key is to work with highly skilled and talented advanced planners who understand the physician's world and are able to identify and implement those strategies that would make a significant financial difference.

Appendix

CHOOSING FINANCIAL ADVISORS WISELY

With Asa Bret Prince

Cautionary Tale #1 | The Case of the Fictitious Hedge Fund

At a hospital fundraiser, a wealthy physician couple were introduced to a "rising star" hedge fund manager. They all got to talking. The hedge fund manager was once a trader at Goldman Sachs—a job he took after getting his M.B.A. from Harvard. Within seven years he was running their proprietary trading desk in London. After about five years at that position, he took his key people and set up his own offshore hedge fund. Because of their cutting-edge proprietary trading strategies he has been able to generate 30 percent returns or better year in and year out, and he has the audited statements from one of the Big Four accounting firms to prove it. Moreover, that 30 percent was after fees.

Thirty-percent returns were much better than the returns the physician couple was getting. Their investment portfolio was consistently beating the S&P 500 by a point or two after fees. They thought this was great, but it was not nearly as good as the consistent returns the hedge fund was getting.

A few weeks later the physicians approached the hedge fund manager to invest in his fund. The minimum investment was $5 million and there was a two-year period where the physicians could not access the monies. Although the minimum was steep and the two-year lock-up was a little long for them, they decided to invest with the hedge fund. But first they wanted proof of the hedge fund's performance.

The hedge fund manager provided "audited" statements of the funds performance, including each and every transaction for the previous eight years—the life of the fund. These documents were handed to the physicians' accountant, who did indeed verify that the transactions in the documents would result in the performance claims of the hedge fund manager.

The physician couple invested $6 million into the hedge fund. The first year they saw a 42 percent return on their investment after fees. In the second year their investment was gone as was the hedge fund manager and all their money.

It turned out that the hedge fund was a fantasy. The hedge fund manager took money from investors and lived well—very well. Because of his exceptional performance on paper, very few investors took money out of his fund. The performance numbers were accurate after-the-fact constructions. It all fell apart when a jilted girlfriend told the police the reality behind the façade, motivating the hedge fund manager to vanish.

The police investigation uncovered that the hedge fund manager never worked for Goldman Sachs nor did he have a Harvard M.B.A. He never held any position in a major financial institution, but he did almost finish high school.

Cautionary Tale #2 | Investing in Rare Clocks and Rarer Watches

His card read *Certified Professional Horologist.* This certification came from the European Association of Horologists. He made his living providing rare collectable watches and other timepieces to wealthy investors. Because of his education, his 25 years of experience in the business, and the panoply of contacts he had cultivated, he was able to act as a purchasing agent for wealthy investors, enabling them to acquire prized possessions at wonderful prices. His core clients were successful physicians.

In about a decade he purchased on behalf of wealthy investors more than $60 million worth of timepieces. He was renowned for being able to find rare and unique items few other dealers or collectors or investors were able to get their hands on. For his services, he received a 5 percent fee based on the cost of the item.

The physician investor, in need of money, took the "rare" timepiece the horologist sold him to Sotheby's, with the thought of having them place it in one of their auctions. It turned out the timepiece was not rare and not very valuable, but it was a very good copy of a rare and valuable clock. This made the physician quite angry, and he took it out directly on the horologist. The physician put him in the hospital with a bunch of broken bones, a broken nose and minus a few teeth. This situation prompted a number of lawsuits that led to the uncovering of the scam.

It turned out that one of the things that made the timepieces he sold so rare and unique was that they were clever forgeries. The horologist was really pretty good at repairing and building clocks and watches. He exploited this skill by doctoring watches and clocks, often attaching high-quality brand names to less austere pieces. This enables him to get not only his 5 percent on a exorbitantly inflated price but to get a price for a timepiece worth less than 10 percent of what he sold it for.

In the end his affluent clients—many of them physicians—were out millions upon millions of dollars. These monies were never recovered as the scam artist loved the good life—as many of them do.

———————————

As we have noted, most people equate the profession of medicine with very solid incomes and substantial personal wealth (see Chapter 8, "Asset-Protection Planning"). The result of these perceptions is that physicians—especially truly affluent physicians—are regularly targeted by corrupt advisors—including scam artists who portray themselves as financial advisors.

There are many times when physicians can trust the financial advisors they are introduced to because of the due diligence conducted by the referral source. For example, if a topflight lawyer recommends a money manager, the lawyer is putting his or her reputation on the line and that should mean the lawyer has validated the integrity of the money manager.

At the same time, we have seen a deluge of situations where affluent physicians fail to, in any way, conduct any form of due diligence on their financial advisors. In Chapter 6, "Caveat Emptor," we saw that 40.4 percent of affluent physicians admitted to being cheated by corrupt advisors. Furthermore, 59.9 percent of affluent physicians were pitched an asset-protection scam.

When an affluent physician is in doubt, before he or she invests, before he or she hands over money to a financial advisor, it's advisable to conduct a background check on the advisor. Quite often the unscrupulous advisor has been plying his or her nefarious trade for some time. Therefore, a little digging can save a lot of money let alone the amount of anxiety and aggravation that can be avoided.

Beyond Vetting Financial Advisors

Increasingly affluent physicians are having background investigations conducted on the financial advisors they employ. From checking credentials to checking investment performance claims, affluent physicians are justifiably becoming more circumspect. No doubt a lot of this has to do with being "burned" or knowing a colleague who was.

We are also seeing more and more background investigations when it comes to:

- The charities affluent physicians donate to
- The people affluent physicians hire who have access to their families and properties
- Proposed business partners

Bogus charities have always been a plague of the wealthy and never more so than today. The same can be said of potential business partners who are looking for seed money. With issues ranging from identity theft to the rare but devastating abduction of a child, affluent physicians, like the wealthy the world over, are becoming more cautious.

Leveraging Negative Migration

Unfortunately, it takes being cheated or something "bad" to happen before most people will take action. What happens is that they end up closing the barn door after the horse has left. However, if there are more horses in the barn, they are making sure those other horses are not leaving.

By using personal security specialists, vetting financial advisors, and making certain their residences are properly secured, affluent physicians are benefiting from the criminal mantra of *negative migration*. Con artists, burglars, rapists, or other criminal types are more inclined to search out the easiest target. So, when an affluent physician has a financial advisor investigated, if that advisor is corrupt he or she will disappear, preferring to find more gullible, less cautious physician prey.

Conclusion

When there is any reasonable doubt (and even unreasonable doubt) about the veracity of a financial advisor's claim, it's critical to verify the claim independently. One way this is accomplished is by bringing in a professional to conduct a background investigation on the people involved.

What is also clear in this more dangerous time is that personal security specialists are becoming a ubiquitous part of the world of the wealthy. And this certainly holds true for affluent physicians.